Maurice Bloomfield

The Salibhadra Carita

A story of conversion to Jaina monkhood

Maurice Bloomfield

The Salibhadra Carita
A story of conversion to Jaina monkhood

ISBN/EAN: 9783741166273

Manufactured in Europe, USA, Canada, Australia, Japa

Cover: Foto ©Andreas Hilbeck / pixelio.de

Manufactured and distributed by brebook publishing software
(www.brebook.com)

Maurice Bloomfield

The Salibhadra Carita

Bloomfield

Śālibhadra Carita

Sir George A. Grierson
with the compliments of
Maurice Bloomfield

Reprint from Journal of the American Oriental Society
Volume 43, pages 257–316

THE ŚĀLIBHADRA CARITA

A Story of Conversion to Jaina Monkhood

Maurice Bloomfield

Johns Hopkins University

The Śālibhadra Carita was composed originally by Dharmakumāra in Vikramasaṁvat 1334 (1277 A. D.). According to the Praśasti, 7. 150 ff., his spiritual descent is from the sect (vaṅśa or gacha) of Nāgendra, thru Hemaprabha, Dharmaghoṣa, Somaprabha, and Vibudhaprabha. Tho his work is said to be the śrīśālilīlākathā, it was apparently not polished enough to suit the taste of the time, and was, therefore, worked over in the highest style of kāvya by Pradyumnasūri (Pradyumnācārya), as is stated in 7. 153:

> iyaṁ kathā vṛddhakumārikeva sadūṣaṇā bhūṣaṇavarjitāsīt,
> pradyumnadevasya paraṁ prasādād babhūva pāṇigrahaṇasya yogyā.

'This tale, like an old maid, was full of faults, and devoid of ornateness; but by the grace of the savant Pradyumna it was rendered fit for marriage.'[1] According to Jacobi, in the Preface to his edition of Pradyumna's Samarādityasaṁkṣepa (Ahmedabad 1906), p. 31, Pradyumna was frequently selected to do poetic rifacimentos of other writers' work. The Managers (vyavasthāpakāḥ) of the Yaśovijayagranthamālā, who print a preface and digest at the beginning of their publication of our text, give

---

[1] A list of publications of the very active Yaśovijaya Jaina Granthamālā (published under the care of His Holiness Shastra Visharad Jainacharya, whose recent death is a great blow to Jainism and Jaina scholarship) is appended to the present text of the Śālibhadra Carita. Under nr. 15, the text is announced as follows: Śrīśālibhadracaritaṁ ṭippaṇasahitaṁ śrīdharmakumārasudhiyā viracitam, apūrvo 'yaṁ kathāgrantho mahākāvyaśabdapratipādyaḥ. A recent leaflet issued as a sūcīpattra of the Śrīyaśovijaya Jaina Granthamālā lists over 100 publications in Sanskrit, Hindī, Marāṭhī, Gujarātī, and English.

a list of texts which thus enjoyed Pradyumna's favor (prasāda). In addition to our Carita they are as follows:

The Mallinātha Mahākāvya (Caritra) by Vinayacandrasūri
The Prabhāvaka Caritra by Prabhācandrasūri
The Upamitibhavaprapañcakakathāsāroddhāra by Devendrasūri
The Kuvalayamālā Kathā by Ratnaprabhasūri
The Upadeśakandalīṭīkā by Bālacandrasūri
The Vivekamañjarīṭīkā by Bālacandrasūri
The Samarādityasaṁkṣepa by Pradyumnācarya
The Śreyāṅsanātha Caritra by Mānatunga.

This list is rather longer than that mentioned by Jacobi, *l. c.*

The editors in the Preface cite the following stanza concerning Pradyumna; it seems to be composed by themselves, in imitation of the fourth stanza of Pradyumna's Praśasti in the Samarādityasaṁkṣepa (p. 415), to wit:

śiṣyaḥ śrīkanakaprabhasya sukaviḥ śrībālacandrānujo
jyāyān śrījayasiṅhataḥ pratibhayā śrīvastupālastutaḥ,
asmadgotramahattaraḥ kaviguruḥ pradyumnasūriprabhur
vidvadvṛndakavitvaśodhanadhanogranthaṁ mudāśodhayat.

According to another stanza (7. 154) in the Praśasti of Śālibhadra the present work was written down at the first inspection (prathamādarśe) by the Gaṇin Prabhāvacandra, the author of the Prabhāvaka Caritra.

The work is published for the first time (apūrva) as Nr. 15 of the series Yaśovijayagranthamālā, by Shah Harakhchand Bhurabai, Benares, Vīrasaṁvat 2436 (A. D. 1910). The text is divided into seven Prakramas (sometimes, irregularly, called Prastāvas), totalling 1171 stanzas. It is, on the whole, well edited; the list of errata (śodhanapatram) is supplemented at the end of this essay.

The scene of this story is Rājagṛha, where rules King Śreṇika with his queen Cellaṇā and his son and minister Abhayakumāra. It is an account of the conversion and salvation of the youthful son of a merchant prince, Śālibhadra, or, for short, Śāli. His father's name is Gobhadra [2]; his mother's Bhadrā; his sister's, Subhadrā. The latter is married to a merchant Dhanya. Gobhadra, tired of earthly futilities, turns ascetic, dies, and is

---

[2] Hence Śāli is also known by the patronymic Gāubhadri.

reborn as a glorious god in the Sāudharma heaven. There, remembering his former birth, he puts himself in touch with his son, and confers upon him wealth and earthly glory, so that Śāli lives in his palace, together with his thirty-two wives, in a state of bliss superior to that of the gods.

Certain merchants from a distance offer to King Śreṇika some magic shawls for so high a price that the king ironically refuses to buy them. They then wait upon Bhadrā, Śāli's mother, who buys the shawls at their full price and presents them to her daughters-in-law. Queen Cellaṇā hears of this, chides the king, and bids him get the shawls by fair means or foul. The king sends his doorkeeper to get the shawls from Bhadrā, but she is unable to deliver the goods which she no longer owns. The doorkeeper reports this, and also that Śāli is living in more than royal pomp. Śreṇika decides to see for himself, and when Śāli beholds him in all his glory, he is seized by the conviction that all existence is worthless, where the highest ruler is a mere living creature, with feet and hands, like himself.

This is pratyekabodhi, as Śāli himself recognizes triumfantly in what is the climax of the story. He compares his enlightenment, to his own advantage, with that of the four classical Pratyekabuddhas, famous both among Buddhists and Jainas. Whereas they were enlightened by the perishable nature of mean or trivial things, Śāli has recognized the futility of life even tho veiled by the splendor of a king in all his glory.

Śāli resorts to the Gaṇin Dharmaghoṣa, by whom he is instructed in the higher religion. Urged on by his growing aversion to the world (vāirāgya) he abandons each day one of his thirty-two wives, so that it would take him thirty-two days to dispose of the lot. This comes to the notice of Dhanya, husband of Subhadrā, Śāli's sister, who is seized by the spirit of the occasion, and exclaims that such shilly-shallying does not ferry one across the sea of desire. In proper course first Dhanya and then Śāli place themselves at the feet of the Holy Lord Vīra; go out as homeless ascetics; return after long wanderings as emaciated monks to Rājagṛha; are not recognized by their mother Bhadrā, but receive their pāraṇa food from Dhanyā, Śāli's mother in his former birth as a shepherd boy, named Saṁgama (see below). They finally die of fast under a tree (pādapopagama) on the Vāibhāra mountain, and are reborn as gods in the Heaven called Sarvārthasiddha.

Śāli's glorious destiny is motivated by the story of his previous birth in which he performs the self-abnegating act of giving alms to a monk who has come to break his fast (pāraṇa). This is told in the first introductory book of the Carita, and not, as is the usual practice, by an omniscient Kevalin who appears at the proper moment at the end of the story, and explains the fortunes of the hero as due to his conduct in a previous birth. Śāli's prenatal predecessor is a shepherd boy, named Saṁgama, son of a poor widowed mother, named Dhanyā. On a certain festal day, when everybody is feasting, she obtains, thru contributions from charitable neighbors, materials for a luscious meal for her boy, also anxious for a feast. Just as he is starting to eat, a Muni who is about to break a month's fast comes along; Saṁgama presents him with his food; and the Muni eats and blesses him. After his death Saṁgama is reborn as Śālibhadra

The text presents itself under the caption of a dānadharmakathā (1.1); more precisely as a dānāvadāna[3] (2.1). In the Jaina system (see our text 3.49; 5.82)[4] dāna figures as one of the four prescripts for the life of a householder (gṛhidharma), namely, dāna, 'giving'; śīla, 'personal virtue'; tapas, 'asceticism'; and bhāva or bhāvanā, 'meditation'. The dāna, in turn, figures under the three heads of jñānadāna, 'conferring knowledge'; abhayadāna, 'conferring security'; and annadāna, 'giving food'. With amazing insistence Jaina texts dwell upon annadāna, especially when it takes the form of breaking the fast of an ascetic (pāraṇa). Our text is presumably the most elaborate and poetic exposition of the glory that ensues upon this last form of generosity. There is, however, scarcely a longer Jaina chronicle

---

[3] Glossed, avadānam atyadbhutaṁ karma. The word avadāna is certainly not ordinary in Jaina literature, but is commonly employed in Sanskrit Buddhist literature (Divyāvadāna, Avadānaśataka etc.) to designate, with tiresome iteration, stories in which the karma accumulated in a certain existence bears fruit, good or evil, in a subsequent life. The word (7.94) vāsīcandana-kalpa, '(ascetic) to whom the (burning) sword and (cooling) sandal are all the same', as I have shown in *JAOS* 40.339 ff. (see below, p. 306), is another of the many technical specialties that connect, in this sfere, Jaina and Buddhist conceptions. So also the four Pratyekabuddhas (p. 275).

[4] Cf. my 'Life of Pārśvanātha', p. 119 note.

which does not contain some account of, or allusion to, the merit of feeding a Yati. In the present text this virtue, displayed in a former birth, leads Śālibhadra on to the attainment of the true ideal of Jainism, the destruction of all karma (kṣīṇa-karma), thru the rigors of asceticism that disregards all suffering, and, finally, death from starvation in a holy spot.

The story is told very briefly and without the least ornateness in Triṣaṣṭiśalākāpuruṣa Caritra, Parvan X = Mahāvīra Caritra 10.57ff. Much later the fertile writer Jinakīrti (about 1438 A. D.) is the author of a Dhanyaśālicaritra, which, doubtless, deals with our theme; see Weber, *Sanskrit- und Prākrit-Handschriften*, vol. ii, p. 1109, note 4; C. M. Duff, *The Chronology of India*, pp. 254 ff. Guerinot, *Essai de Bibliographie Jaina*, no. 402 (p. 199), registers a Jaina Gujarātī tale, entitled Śālibhadra Śāhno Rās (published in Bombay, 1889).

In a tangled form, the events of our Carita are retold in Kathākośa, pp. 78 ff. of Tawney's Translation, and, partly, in the Āvaśyaka Tales; see Leumann, as reported by Tawney, *ib.* p. 238. In Kathākośa the name of the hero is Dhanya, both in the pre-birth and in the present-day stories. In the Āvaśyaka tale the pre-birth story is told with Dhanya as its hero. The same rebirth story occurs also as the story of Sthāvara and his mother, at the end of Jñānasāgara's story of Ratnacūḍa; see Hertel, *Indische Erzähler*, vol. vii, pp. 165 ff. (Leipzig, 1922).

Otherwise also the worthies of the story, Gobhadra, Bhadrā, Śālibhadra, and Dhanya, have a certain standing in Jaina tradition. Anent Gobhadra a gloss at Śālibhadra Carita 3. 71 quotes the following Prākrit śloka:

jena kayaṁ sāmannaṁ chammāse jhānasaṁjamaraeṇa,
taṁ munim udārakittiṁ gobhaddarisiṁ namassāmi.

'I revere that Rishi Gobhadra, the Muni of exalted reputation, who, devoted to contemplation and restraint, performed asceticism for a period of six months.'

'Rich as Śālibhadra', is a Jaina way of saying, 'Rich as Croesus'; see Hemavijaya's Kathāratnākara, story 3. Very definite is the allusion in Siṁhāsanadvātriṁśikā (Weber, *Indische Studien*, 15. 291) to our Śālibhadra as 'the son of the merchant-princess Bhadrā, who enjoyed the youthful aroma of his thirty-two wives.' Identical with our Dhanya is, probably, that Dhanya who along with his two wives is converted to the Jaina faith in Caritrasundara's Mahīpāla Carita; see Hertel, 'Jinakīrti's Geschichte von Pāla und Gopāla,' *BKSGW*, 1917, p. 19. A faint echo of our story is the mention of the farmer Bhadra in Śāligrāma, most generous to the poor (dīnadānaparāyaṇaḥ), in Mallinātha Caritra 2. 342. Śāli and the events of his life have, presumably, a historical kernel.

The text, in its final form, is written in the highest style of mahākāvya, governed by the extremest habits of Hindu rhetoric (alaṁkāra). To a Western reader its style, turgid, allusive, full of puns, alliterations, and double ententes, seems artificial or eufuistic. Aside from familiar devices, such as kalā in the double sense of 'accomplishment' and 'fase of the moon' (5. 75), or the equally standard puns on guṇa and vaṅśa (1. 16; 5. 54), the text goes far in the direction of independent tours-de-force. In 1. 31 dehe occurs in three different meanings: (saṁ-)dehe, 'doubt'; dehe, 'burnt'; and dehe, 'in the body'. In 2. 13 the word vaśā occurs in vaśāsthūlāḥ (sc. gāvaḥ), 'sleek with fat'; suvaśāḥ, 'good kine'; vaśāḥ (glossed, vaśyāḥ), 'subjected to'; and vaśādoṣadūṣitāḥ (glossed, vandhyādoṣadūṣitāḥ) 'free from the blemish of sterility'. In 2. 77 reṇur means once 'dust', and once 'they jingled' (gloss, śabdaṁ cakruḥ). In 3. 51 the two syllables mātrā occur thrice, in the senses of 'with mother', 'measure', and 'not hither'. Yet more artificially, 3. 6, mudvahe nyasya tadbhāram udvahe vratam udvahe, 'having unloaded the burden of that upon my joy-bestowing son, I shall take upon myself the holy vow', where the syllables mudvahe occur in three different senses.

Examples of double meaning (śleṣa) of one and the same syllables (indicated by the word pakṣe in the gloss) are 1. 15, bahudhānyopakāraka = bahudhā + anyo°, 'in many ways benefiting others', or bahu-dhānya + upakāraka, 'benefiting with much grain', said of a village. In 1. 22 kulīna means 'of good family', and 'clinging to the earth' (ku-līna); aviparīta, 'traveled by birds' (avi-parīta) and 'not perverse' (a-viparīta); vipattra, 'protecting against misfortune' (vipat-tra) and 'wingless' (vi-pattra). Not infrequently precise fonetics are disregarded. Thus in 5. 44 bindu means 'drop' and 'knowing' (vindu); in 5. 150 śāradīna, 'autumnal', alliterates with sāradīnatā, 'essential pusillanimity'; in 7.122 mahāśamarasaṁraṁbhe is either mahāsamara-saṁrambhe 'in great conflict', or mahā-śama-rasaṁ rambhe 'essence of great asceticism, O Rambhā'. There is scarcely a stanza in the entire poem free from such rhetorical devices, some of which are pretty certain to occur in other texts of this class.

The following digest (uddhāra) of this Carita is made with reference to the events of the story and the skilful depiction of the characters in it, rather than the somewhat eufuistic diction which suits native, rather than Western, literary habits.

DIGEST OF THE STORY OF ŚĀLIBHADRA

First Prakrama: The Story of Saṁgama, the pious shepherd boy (pre-birth of Śālibhadra).

Introductory stanzas extol the wish-tree (kalpadru) of the virtue of almsgiving (dānadharma), one of the stated items of Jaina religion[5]; invoke the protection of Nābheya (= Ṛṣabha), the first Arhat, famous for his liberality[6]; of Vīra, the last Arhat, 'the tree of whose wisdom, rooted in his great liberality during his first birth, has not been uprooted by the mighty elefant False Doctrine'; and, finally, of gāur devī sarasvatī.[7] The favor of the spiritual ancestors of the author Dharmakumāra, namely the Śrīsomaprabhasūrayaḥ, is next bespoken, 'at the touch of whose hands (rays) there is an outburst of taste (water) from me who am a stone';[8] strength is asked for the redactor (śuddhakṛt)[9] Śrīpradyumna, pupil of Śrīkanakaprabha, himself pupil of Śrīdevānanda; and, lastly, praise is bespoken from the Śrīmadudayaprabhasūrayaḥ[10]. The Story of Śrīśālibhadra is then announced.

The first chapter (prakrama) contains an account of Śālibha-

---

[5] Defined, rather narrowly, in a gloss on dānadharma, at 7.148: dānarūpo māsopavāsinaḥ yateḥ kṣīradānadharmaḥ.

[6] ādāu dhanabhave yena ghṛtameghāyitam.

[7] Meaning here, vāk sarasvatī, 'the goddess of speech'.

[8] The moonstone, touched by the rays of the moon, yields water.

[9] The jejune work of the original author, Dharmakumāra, was adorned, i. e. turned into Kāvya poetry, by Pradyumna; see 7.153, 156, and the stanza at the bottom of p. 1 of the Sanskrit introduction to the text.

[10] Udayaprabhasūri (about 1230 A. D.) is the author of Dharmābhyudaya Mahākāvya, or Saṁghapati Carita; see Guerinot, *Essai de Bibliographie Jaina*, pp. 79, 398.

dra's existence in a former birth as the saintly youth Saṁgama.[11] The scene is laid in the lovely and prosperous village of Śāligrāma in the country of Magadha. The curtain rises upon the poor and virtuous widow Dhanyā, who is bringing up her beautiful orfan boy, Saṁgama. He does not even know the name of his father. By hard chores, such as scrubbing and pounding grain in rich men's houses, she supports her son and herself. At eight years of age Saṁgama becomes a shepherd. By contemplating the Sun (or the Arhat)[12], he is led to abandon the tyranny of his senses, and becomes enlightened. In the manner of a Sādhu, with staff and piece of cloth as a garment, his belly his only provision on the way[13], he herds his calves in the woods outside the village, and passes his time in devotion to the (eight) Mothers (37).[14]

It happens that Saṁgama, accustomed to rough food, notices on a certain festival day, that delicacies are being consumed in every house but his own. As tho he were the son of a rich man, not sensing the proprieties of the situation, he asks his mother, politely to be sure, to prepare for him at once a pudding with sugar and milk. Dhanyā, realizing that Saṁgama can not have evil inclinations, promises to supply him with a feast, but she finds that she has not the means. She bewails her low estate of woman and widow, and complains to her father and mother (both dead) that she whose name is Dhanyā, 'Wealthy', is unable to provide her only son even a single feast (51).

The women of the neighborhood, disposed to be friendly, ask the cause of her grief. Dhanyā avows that she is not grieving for herself, but for her son whose desire, she says with self-persiflage, she is unable to gratify. 'To-day my son, as charioteer, ignorantly hitched me, an old cow, to the chariot of his desire.'[15] She then tells them what she needs, and the women, severally, send her the ingredients for a feast, rejoicing the heart of Dhanyā

---

[11] In a gloss at 1.35 he is called Saṁgamaka; also later in the text itself, 2.48.

[12] jaganmitrāvalokena, glossed, sūryo 'rhaṅś ca.

[13] kukṣiśambalī: may perhaps mean, 'all his provision being in his belly'.

[14] mītṛbhaktibhāk, glossed, aṣṭāu mātaraḥ; cf. 5.65. The 'Mothers' are doubtless intended in Prabandhacintāmaṇi, p. 182.

[15] manorathārathe 'dya mām avedanaḥ sutaḥ sūtaḥ saṁyuyoja jaradgavīm.

(73). Saṁgama leaves his calves in the forest, bathes, and returns home. Dhanyā gladly serves him the pudding she has prepared, and then goes away in superstitious dread of looking on him with delight[16] (82). Along comes, like a wish-jewel, or the heavenly wish-tree, a great ascetic (yati) who is about to break a month's feast. His brilliant presence in so humble a village suggests striking fenomena of nature and mythological events, such as Indra's elefant coming down to earth, or the Gañgā flowing in the jungle, or the paradise-tree growing in the desert.[17] Saṁgama realizes his opportunity, and determines to make the occasion redound to his spiritual advantage. With the hair of his body bristling with joy, he addresses the Muni in words of ecstatic praise of the latter's virtues and beneficent power. In a state of supreme love (bhakti) he hands him his own dish (109). The Yati, weak from fast, comes to himself, accepts the food, blesses Saṁgama, and returns to his abode (111). Mother Dhanyā, returning from another house, not knowing what had happened in between, sets other food before him. This he eats, rinses his mouth, and, as tho he had reached the glory of a king, enters into a state of bliss (116).

The rest of the chapter (prakrama) does not really advance the story. Sts. 117–135 are devoted to praise of the virtue of alms-giving (dānaśīla), reinforced by sundry historical or legendary allusions to former dānas, placed by the side of Saṁgama's act. In these figure the Savior Śreyāṅsa, grandson of Nābheya (Ṛṣabha); the Princess Candanā[18] who gratified

---

[16] saṁtoṣadṛgbhayāt; comm. dṛṣṭilaganabhayāt; see Appendix iii.

[17] āirāvaṇo 'yaṁ bhūpīṭhe gañgāpūraś ca jañgale,
marāu jātaḥ pārijātaḥ sādhur grāme yad īdṛśe (90).

[18] A quaint story, Mallinātha Caritra 7.1023 ff., tells how Candanā gave the Lord Vīra his pāraṇa, to wit: King Śatānīka attacks King Dadhivāhana of Campā, who flees afright, abandoning his queen Dhāriṇī and her lovely daughter Vasumatī. Śatānīka makes Dhāriṇī his chief queen, but decides to sell her daughter as a slave, in open market. As Vasumatī stands there, grass on her head as a sign of slavehood, a rich merchant, Dhanavāha, noting her grace and nobility, asks what is her descent and name, but she remains silent, too proud to make an appeal. Dhanavāha takes her home to his wife Mūlā, and she lives with the pair as a cherished daughter, under the name of Candanā.

She, nevertheless, incurs the jealousy of her foster-mother Mūlā. Once,

Lord Vīra[19], and the notorious Mūladeva, who has been canonized, as it were, by the Jains, as, perhaps, the most imposing example of the virtue of dāna (130)[20]. The text continues with reflections on Saṁgama's great act, which is sure to redound to his advantage at rebirth, even if the gods did not shower this world's goods upon him in his present existence (133)[21]. Unsuspected of spiritual greatness, of humble family, disregarded by illusion (Māra),

---

there being no slave available, Candanā washes the feet of Dhanavāha; during this act of filial regard her beautiful braid falls to the dusty earth; Dhanavāha lifts it up with his staff; Mūlā is confirmed in her jealousy, and decides to cut her off at the root like a poisonous creeper. When her husband goes to his business, she gets a barber to shave off Candanā's hair; beats her; chains her with strong fetters; and throws her into the cellar of the house. She threatens her servants: any one who tells will become a sacrifice in the fire of her anger. In the evening Dhanavāha returns and asks where his daughter is. All are silent, but an old maid-servant, thinking pitifully that her days are short, and that Candanā will perish from grief, points to the carcer where Candanā is confined. He breaks open its door and sees Candanā starved, wilted, fettered like a she-elefant, bald as a nun. He goes to the kitchen but finds there no food, only a little coarse rice collected in the corner of a winnowing-basket. He tells her to eat that, until he returns with a blacksmith to cut her fetters.

Candanā stands there, reflecting that it would be better to give this coarse food to a guest, rather than that she, a princess, should eat it. It happens that the Holy Mahāvīra is wandering about the city for alms. Candanā, fettered, winnowing-basket in hand, manages to place one foot outside the threshold of the house while the other remains inside. In deep piety she offers the rice to Vīra, who, recognizing her purpose, stretches out his hand to receive it.

The gods come to the spot and acclaim her generous gift. They break her fetters like a rotten rope. Her pretty braid is again upon her head, and she appears dressed as a princess. All-knowing wisdom (kevalajñāna) comes to Candanā; she turns nun; in due time she will reach nirvāṇa.

In Mahāvīra's biografy, Kalpasūtra 5.135, Candanā appears at the head of 36,100 nuns in Mahāvīra's following. — Other cases of blissful dānas are cited in my 'Life of Pārśvanātha', p. 128, note 28.

[19] prabhur; comm. śrīvīraḥ.

[20] See especially the excellent study of Professor Pavolini in *Giornale della Società Asiatica Italiana*, 9. 175 ff. Other treatments and other matters pertaining to this subject are discussed in my article, 'The Character and Adventures of Mūladeva', *Proceedings of the American Philosophical Society*, 1913, vol. 52, pp. 616 ff. Mūladeva, as the result of his deed, becomes King of Beṇṇāyaḍa.

[21] mahādāne 'pi yat tasya na surā vavṛṣur vasu,
dātuṁ kila vyalambanta tat prabhūtaṁ bhavāntare.

he has reached enlightenment (135). Next, description of the boy's mood and conduct when taken with his religious fervor: 'Regularly he used to remember, in his mother's absence to cry out in grief, "Alas, mother, (where art thou)?" But, at the contemplation of the Muni, she, in turn, was forgotten.' Under ordinary circumstances even a thorn disturbs one's piety, but now danger to life does not disturb his spirit. The great virtue of renouncing his food for another filled his own mouth with camfor, 'for what was he, a mere shepherd boy, compared with the Muni, a great Indra, crested with flowers?' (143) In sundry other ways he continues to reflect upon the superlative qualities of the Muni and upon the perfect way in which he has achieved dānaśīla: 'Having constituted me an eater of others' food (parānna), my mother set before me a superb meal (paramānna). But I did set out food of the highest goal (paramārthānna), having, forsooth, attended to my own interests' (145). 'Now fitly this distinguished Muni may become for me a pool of the ambrosia of calm, an ever reliable refuge of peace' (146). The honored Mahātman, exemplar of noble men, beautiful as a jeweled mirror, is reflected in Saṁgama, tho he be worthless. Saṁgama's mind is immersed in the nectar-pot of meditation [22] which reaches to his throat; he abandons life thru fast; and enters that very day the pious state that results in complete perfection (160).

iti śālibhadrakathāyāṁ prathamaḥ prakramaḥ samāptaḥ.

Second Prakrama: Birth and marriage of Śālibhadra.

The scene changes from the village of Śāligrāma to the city of Rājagṛha in the land of Magadha in Jambūdvīpa, all of which places are described at length in the conventional, florid style practised by Kāvya writers, especially in connection with geografical and person names. There rules the glorious and pious king Śreṇika (Bimbisāra), familiar to both Buddhist and Jaina legend. Śreṇika is blessed with a perfect wife, Cellaṇā, and an intellectual son, prince Abhayakumāra, who acts as his minister [23]

---

[22] samādhāna=samādhi.

[23] All three are mentioned together (Cellaṇā as Cillaṇā) in Kathākośa, pp. 175 ff.; Hemavijaya's Kathāratnākara, story 82; Śreṇika and Abhaya figure much in Rāuhiṇeya Caritra; in Hemavijaya, stories 85, 176; in Hema-

(36). In the same capital lives a merchant-prince Gobhadra, with his wife Bhadrā, sunk in the depths of connubial bliss (47). The soul of Saṁgama, in the fulness of time, descends into the womb of Bhadrā. She sees in a dream a field of ripe rice which looks as tho it had come from Śāligrāma ('Rice-village') [24]; reports the dream to her husband; and is told that she is big with a son. She is taken with a pregnant woman's desire (dohada), in this instance, desire to give alms, [25] in which desire her husband supports her loyally.

At the end of nine months she gives birth to a son (63). All the town joins in his birth-festival; the child is given the name Śālibhadra (to match the dream, as well as the names of his parents); and he is put in charge of reliable nurses. Every stage of his development, such as crawling, [26] walking, eating, talking, furnishes his father occasion for sacramental celebrations. As a child he plays about with animal companions, dressed in baby finery, a joy to his parents (82). 'Some children are filthy as swine; some, frisky as monkeys; some croak weirdly like frogs; and some are like wild elefants. Śāli, however, loves cleanliness like a high-bred horse; is clean-limbed as a tortoise; mighty as a lion; and pure as an ascetic.' [27] He is in due time made over to a noble teacher by whom he is instructed in the 72 accomplishments (kalāḥ) of a young gentleman (87).

Śālibhadra reaches young manhood in a marvelous state of beaúty, which gives rise to a detailed comparison of his every part with the correspondingly beautiful things in nature. 'Afraid of the overpowering lustre of his body, the yellow-blossomed pandamus arranges to protect itself, as it were, by a hedge of thorns' (92). His every part is described painstakingly: feet, legs, navel, heart, arms, hands, throat, teeth, cheeks, face, brow,

---

candra's Commentary on Yogaśāstra 2.114; Śreṇika and Celanā (!) in Mahāvīra Carita 10.90; etc. Cf. Weber, Samyaktva-Kāumudī, p. 12.

[24] Allusion to the soul's former home, which, by the terms of its name, is supposed to abound in rice-fields. For dreams that foretell the birth of a noble child, see my 'Life of Pārśvanātha', p. 189 ff. Such dreams are known as mahāsvapna, 'great-dream'.

[25] See the author, *JAOS* 40.1 ff., especially 17 ff.

[26] riṅṣaṇam, text, for riñkhaṇam; see Appendix vi.

[27] puriṣaśūkarāḥ kecic cāpalyakapayaḥ pare, māyugomāyavaḥ ke 'pi bālā vyālā ivetare, pāvitryaprītijātyāśvaḥ saṁlīnāñgatvakacchapaḥ, sa tu siṅha ivāujasvī śamavān śamavān iva.

eyes, forehead, and hair. In a final burst of ecstasy his beauty is said to excel that of other men, to be equal to that of the gods, and to be highly admired by the Nāga maidens dwelling in the lower world (Pātāla). In addition, dāna (alms-giving), the most distinguished among virtues,[28] like pāyasa (pudding) among foods, makes Śālibhadra shine as prince among young men (113).

Father Gobhadra, seeing his son such a paragon, chooses for him 32 beautiful maidens of Rājagṛha, as tho they were four times eight picked from the eight crores of heavenly women. They are accomplished, of good family, and all their bodily parts are like the lotus[29], matching Śālibhadra's perfections. Following brilliant marriage festivities, Śālibhadra lives with his wives devoted by day and by night to the pleasures of the senses, a veritable elefant among women (140).[30]

iti śrīśālibhadracarite janmavivāhavarṇano nāma dvitīyaḥ prakramaḥ.

Third Prakrama:

Gobhadra turns ascetic, dies, and becomes a god. He returns to shower blessings upon Śālibhadra, in which the six seasons cooperate with him.

Gobhadra regards the perfections of his son as a good omen, pointing to the fulfilment of his own career. Whereas some sons like gambling, rifle one's property, or, like an overdue debt, bring sorrow, others, gifted with the virtues of the golden age, afford success and joy, as tho they constituted uncounted merit (puṇya). 'Now that son of mine is like a black wish-jewel[31] for increase of fortune, an antidote against sorrow, a joy to the coral-tree of the law.' Gobhadra decides to unload the burden of householdership upon this son of a lovely mother[32], and to take the vow: 'When there is a beautiful, beloved son, acknow-

---

[28] Carried over from his pre-birth as Saṁgama who gained merit (puṇya) by feeding the ascetic (p. 265).

[29] They are, in fact, padminī.

[30] nārīkuñjaratāṁ yāti.

[31] kṛṣṇacitrakaḥ, glossed by, kālī cintāmaṇiḥ; previously (1.85), kṛṣṇaś citrakaḥ.

[32] bhādramātura, apparently only in Pāṇini, with pun on the name of his mother Bhadrā; see Appendix iv.

ledged to be a region-elefant, (the father) who does not desert the householder's desire verily is a cattle-herd.'[33] (7). Just as his thoughts are turning to Vīra, the park-keeper announces the arrival of that Holy Saint himself. Gobhadra with a select retinue goes to honor Vardhamāna on Mount Vāibhāra and listens to a sermon of his on saṁsāra. Gobhadra is inspired to devote himself to pure religion[34]. Returning to his wife, he extols her many graces and virtues, which have led him on the way to religion, and requests her consent to his undergoing the dīkṣā with the Lord Vīra, in order that he may obtain the fourth and greatest purpose of life[35] (22). Bhadrā remonstrates tearfully; she is weak, and has but a single son: will he abandon them both? In such case, is not staying at home more meritorious than the monk's vow? 'The male elefant may rudely spurn the lotus[36] which clings to his feet, but how can even the most restive elefant cast off the spots on his face and trunk[37] which are born on his body[38]?' (27). After other arguments involving figurative, punning, or alliterative exhibits of no mean quality, she clinches her argument by the dogma that a true man is the one to uphold the family, not woman, weak and ignorant by name and nature (30).

Gobhadra retorts that she has, after all, her son to protect her; that merit (puṇya) is the essential at the two ends (beginning and end) of existence, man's undertakings in between being non-essential; that religion (dharma) seeks no opportunity against man, whereas death ever lurks; that contempt for a child is

---

[33] supratīke sati prīte pratīte diggaje 'ṅgaje, nāiśānīm yas tyajaty āśāṁ satyaṁ paśupatiḥ sa tu. The verse is a no more than usual example of the double entente style of the entire text: supratīka, in addition to meaning 'beautiful', is also the proper name of a region-elefant; āiśānī āśā means both 'householder's desire', and, 'Śiva's quarter, the north-east'; and paśupati means both 'cattle-herd', and 'Śiva'.

[34] śuklapākṣikatvena dharmamānasam ānaśe.

[35] This is mokṣa, 'release', the three others being dharma, 'religion'; artha, 'property'; and kāma, 'love'. Cf. Vasupūjya Carita 4.8 ff.; Ratnacūḍa (Hertel's Translation, p. 169); our Carita in the gloss to 2.112.

[36] padminī, with double entente, 'female elefant'; so according to the Lexicografers.

[37] padma, to pun with padminī.

[38] aṅgaja with pun on the meaning 'son'.

ınbecoming in the wise.[39] The conclusion to be drawn is hat, strong in her son, she should help her husband to fulfil ıis high purpose (39). Bhadrā is silenced by her husband's ırgument. They both call on Śālibhadra, who receives them in ;reat state, and with the reverence becoming in a son (44). Гhe father now addresses his son, who is seated on his lap, as ın intelligent being of strong character. He points out that iālibhadra, as his noble successor, must undertake the life of ı pious householder with its three stages of childhood, youth ınd old age, devoted to the fourfold dharma[40]. He, Gobhadra, ın the other hand, must prepare himself for victory over the :nemy of Bhāva (pious meditation). Having wisely crossed he sorrowful river of householdership, in the company of Śāli-ıhadra's mother, he is now asking her for the ferry-money, i. e., ıresumably, the price to be paid for release from the further esponsibilities of householdership (52).

Śālibhadra, for his part, objects to his father's unloading the esponsibility of a head of a family upon himself, a mere child. Having yourself cut the snare of saṁsāra, like the fish Rohita[41],) father, will you go away and abandon us that are afright, ust where we are?' (56). But Gobhadra insists that it is Śāli-ıhadra's duty to promote his spiritual efforts, if for no other eason, because a father's glory in heaven confers honor upon he son. Turning to his wife Bhadrā, he bids her show true ove to her son thru firm resolution, and, supported by her hirty-two daughters-in-law, keep up his household. After :ight days' ceremonies preparatory to his niṣkramaṇa[42], Go-ıhadra takes the vow at Lord Vīra's hand; accumulates great nerit thru ascetic practice; dies from fast; and is reborn as a ;od (sura) in the Sāudharma heaven[43] (72).

Up in heaven Gobhadra puts himself into rapport with his on. He remembers that, whereas he himself is a warrior, strong

---

[39] See under proverbs below, Appendix i.

[40] dāna-śīla-tapo-bhāva-catuḥśālena śālitaḥ.

[41] Text, rohitamatsyas, glossed, matsyarājas tu rohitaḥ. Conversely, he fish Taṇḍula, owing to his guilt in eating other fish, goes to the seventh ıell, Bhāvadevasūri's Pārśvanātha Caritra 3.393.

[42] The solemn act of going out from home to homelessness.

[43] Gobhadra seems to have high standing in Jaina tradition according o the Prākrit śloka, quoted on p. 261.

in his reliance upon the Jina, his son has been left behind to fight the battle of life, with only his mother to stand by him. He decides to quench Śāli's sorrows with an ambrosia shower from his own heavenly world. He leaves behind his glorious state, and visits his son (83), bringing with him, as presents to himself and wives, diadems, garments fine-spun as tho made of the rays of the moon, unguents made from sandal, and wreaths made of the flowers of mandāra, the coral-tree of paradise (87). Śāli obtains from his father divine grace and beauty that ever renews itself; his affairs prosper of themselves, being, in this and other regards, superior to the gods who must call their minds into action before they can accomplish anything (104). 'The Lords of the World (bhuvanādhīśvarāḥ), in comparison with Śālibhadra, take demonic (asura) character, whereas the inhabitants of Hell are doubly lowered by him' (105). The gods, in Jaina classification [44] (bhuvanādhīśvara, vyantara, jyotiṣka, vāimānika), are separately shown to be inferior to Śālibhadra (109). He gives alms on an unheard-of scale of liberality (112). His 32 large-eyes wives afford him connubial bliss to a degree commensurate with his virtues (117). The happiness which is enjoyed by both mortals and immortals, superior to the whole world, comes to him, of all others, just as, e. g., wisdom and skill to a minister, or the rivers Gaṅgā and Sindhu to the great ocean (120). The seasons [45] show him love, extol him and cater to his pleasures. For instance, in summer, 'The mountains, beholding the world in the flashes of lightning, roar, as it were, in thunderous voice: "There is no one on the stool of the earth like in beauty to Śāli" ' (134). Or, 'In winter when the sun's glory is dimmed by snowfalls, the sun of Śāli's happiness is in no wise diminished' (145). And so, in their order, all the seasons pleasure him, who is rich in virtue, just as virtues bring happiness to a great monarch, or holy vows to a great ascetic (154).

iti śrīśālibhadracarite gobhadrāgamanaṛtuṣaṭkavarṇano nāma tṛtīyaḥ prakramaḥ.

---

[44] Cf. Hertel, *Pariśiṣṭaparvan*, pp. 14 ff.

[45] The following type of description, referred to as ṛtuṣaṭkavarṇana in the colofon to this chapter, is also known as ṣaḍṛtuvarṇana, each meaning 'description of the six seasons'; see Hemavijaya's Kathāratnākara, story 72 end.

Fourth Prakrama: The magic shawls; King Śreṇika visits Śālibhadra; Śālibhadra's enlightenment (pratyekabodhi).

To the city of Rājagṛha come from another country certain merchants with their goods. They first present themselves to King Śreṇika. The King asks them whence they have come with their honest ware[46]. They reply that they are from the country where rules King Nepāla, and have with them a stock of rare shawls[47], which they wish to dispose of to the King. These garments are warm in winter, cool in summer, delicate as śirīṣa blossoms, and of enormous size. Thereupon they exhibit their precious wares to the King, as poets exhibit their compositions to a connoisseur (14). The King asks for some tangible proof of their value and is told that in winter a brass pot full of butter melts when enveloped in one of them, but that the same garment, in the noon-heat, makes a pot of ghee freeze. The King then asks the price and the merchants demand a lakh of gold. In amazement he retorts that, with such a sum, one may collect elefants, horses, and men, that will ensure victory in battle; but what power has a mere garment? The queen (Cellaṇā), joining the king unexpectedly, crushes the merchants' hope of doing business by spurning these jewels of garments, as being of no more use than a bull's dew-lap. Thereupon the merchants go to the abode of Śālibhadra (25).

His mother Bhadrā, having elicited by questions the virtues of the garments, buys them, eight in number, at their original price, cuts them up, and distributes the pieces among her 32 daughters-in-law, as foot-rugs. They, in turn, place them under Śāli's feet (31). Bhadrā's generosity elicits a group of proverbial stanzas on the relation of mothers-in-law to daughters-in-law: 'Some mothers-in-law and daughters-in-law, by nature wind and gall[48], as it were (in the same body), live in strife with one another, and act like co-wives (in quarrel)'. Under pretense of friendship, they carry on, in their own interest, intrigues, such as are customary in the seraglio of a minister (44).

In the meantime Cellaṇā, King Śreṇika's queen, learns from the gossip of her tire-women what had happened in the matter

---

[46] akāṇakrītakrayāṇakāḥ; see Appendix ii.

[47] ratnakambalaśambalāḥ.

[48] Emend vāttapittaprakṛtī to vāta°.

of the wonderful shawls. She chides the king for not having acquired them, and asks him to take them by force. The king sends a confidential servant to the merchants to demand the garments, but they inform him that Bhadrā, Śāli's mother, has secured them. When this answer is brought to the king, he, mindful of his earlier money scruples, determines to gratify the queen's desire. He sends a door-keeper to Bhadrā to obtain the garments at their proper price. Bhadrā tells him that, tho neither price nor reluctance to part with the treasure counts when the king commands, she is unable to comply with the king's request, because she has already presented the shawls to her daughters-in-law (66). The door-keeper, wondering what sort of people Śāli and his wives may be, reports to the king that Śāli is living in more than royal pomp, and that his mother has distributed the costly garments among her daughters-in-law. The queen's ironic importunities have the effect of weaving Śāli's image into the king's soul; he sends his door-keeper a second time to Śāli's palace with an invitation to wait upon the king. Bhadrā, his mother, goes instead, and tells the king that her son does not leave the top of his palace even to visit his pleasure grove, any more than, for instance, Religion (dharma) leaves Āryadeśa (orthodox India). She, in turn, invites the king to grace her house with his presence; the king accepts the invitation. She arranges her palace for lavish hospitality. The king arrives, is received in state, and seats himself upon a jeweled throne (112).

Bhadrā tells her son that the king has come, but he says absent-mindedly: 'Look over the ware, weigh it, pay for it, and take it.'[49] Bhadrā, delighted, exclaims that she is the most fortunate of women, because her son is so deeply immersed in pleasure[50] as to misunderstand a plain statement. She replies that the king is present in all his majesty. 'The report, "It is the king!", tho of one foot (i. e. one word), enters marvelously the root of Śāli's ear, like a centipede ('hundred-foot'), and brings him to repentance' (120). Śāli reflects that even the strong are of no account: that existence itself is destruction,

---

[49] Śāli's misunderstanding seems to me founded upon a pun between śreṇika and krayāṇaka; his mother says the former; he hears the latter. Similarly Mahāvīracarita 10.106.

[50] līlāgarbheśvaraḥ.

where the highest ruler is a mere living creature with feet and hands like himself (121). The idea that such a king is of no consequence is turned into a pratyekabodhi motif,[51] i. e., it becomes for Śāli, uninstructed, the particular occasion for spiritual insight: 'Of him that wears the shape of a mere bubble in the ocean of saṁsāra, how much is his princehood valued by the wise? Out upon this non-existing glory which has no more permanent habitat than a wandering harlot'. 'I know that the Lord of the three worlds, holy Vīra, is my refuge; what use have I then for this eunuch king of a chess-board?' One is a real king only thru great virtue; what other king can then prevail against him? (128).

As if to clinch his own enlightenment by a particular event (pratyekabodhi), he recalls the four classical pratyekabuddhas, famous alike both among Buddhists and Jains. 'The world-disgust (vāirāgya) of the king of Kaliṅga (Karakaṇḍu), why was it based upon (the spectacle of) a feeble bull?'[52] And he contrasts (to his own advantage) the depressing circumstances of all the four Pratyekabuddhas' enlightenment with his own, which is occasioned by *a king in all his glory*—one might suppose a sight the reverse of depressing: Śāli's vāirāgya has mounted 'like a warrior equipped for battle upon the *king-elefant*' (130).

'Because the king of Pāñcāla (Dommuha, Durmukha) saw a fallen flag, he became disaffected (with the world); but this (Śāli) *saw the king* aloft in shining joy and serenity (and became disaffected)' (131).

'By way of a bracelet Nami's vāirāgya came and was established, but Śāli's vāirāgya came even *by way of the king*' (132).

'The saṁvega (spiritual awakening) of Naggati[53] was incited

---

[51] For pratyekabodhi see my 'Life and Stories of the Jaina Savior Pārśvanātha', pp. 5, 116 note. An additional instance of this mode of conversion by a particular (single) event, in Prabandhacintāmaṇi, p. 29. In Umāsvāti's Tattvārthādhigama Sūtra 10.7 the pratyekabuddha is fitly contrasted with the bodhita: the first is enlightened by himself, the second by the instruction of another.

[52] A śloka similar to the Prākrit in Jacobi, *Ausgewählte Erzählungen*, p. 38 bottom, is quoted in the gloss: śvetaṁ sujātaṁ suvibhaktaśṛṅgaṁ goṣṭhāṅgane vīkṣya vṛṣaṁ jarārtam, ṛddhiṁ tv anṛddhiṁ (text, tvaṛddhiṁ) prasamīkṣya bodhāt kaliṅgarājarṣir avāpa dharmam.

[53] For the form of this word see Appendix ii.

like a veritable kokila bird, when he came upon the fallen fruit of a mango-tree, but this man-lion's (Śāli's) saṁvega rose, lion-fashion, when he *came upon the king*' (133).

Tho Śāli now, like one of true faith, looks upon Śreṇika as the unwelcome sight of error, he respects his mother's wish, and descends with his wives from the seventh story of his palace to pay his respects. The king is delighted with him, embraces him, and, amorously [54], sets him upon his hip. The king enjoys the highest bliss from this contact, whereas Śāli breaks into tears (140). Bhadrā tells the king that Śāli, accustomed to heavenly wreaths, clothes, food, and unguents, furnished him by his father, who is a god in heaven, abhors exceedingly men's breath.[55] She begs him to let go Śāli, who is the pet of Fortune, and tender as a lotus [56]. The King releases Śāli who again retires with his wives to the upper terrace of his palace (145).

Now Bhadrā orders a grand shampoo for the king. As he is being finally rinsed, his signet ring falls into the water, 'like a beloved mistress in her tantrums, when she has become subject to anger and pride.' The king is annoyed by the loss, but when, at Bhadrā's order, the water is drawn off by a servant-maid, he easily sees the ring in the bath. 'Like a villager in the midst of city-folk, like a coward in the midst of heroes, [57] like a pauper in the midst of the rich, like a fool in the midst of the wise, it seems now a lustreless thing among jewels' [58] (156). This chills his love for Śāli, tho, at the same time, he recognizes his superior character. With play upon Śāli's name ('Rice'), he exclaims: 'While we, 'Barley' [59], having fallen from our place, must endure splitting and other treatment of grain, 'Rice' (Śāli) alone of all

[54] This is, perhaps, what seems to be intended by the expression tam ...bhūbhṛd utsaṅgaraṅge raṅgān nyavīviśat. The Digest parafrases, svotsaṅge taṁ śālim nidhāyācikrīḍat. Cf., later on in the digest, Śāli's thought, mayy api hanta svāmī vartate (p. 4, l.6 from bottom).

[55] naraśvāsavyāsāir dodūyatetarām.

[56] The scholiast remarks that lotuses are crushed (indiff rently) either by the hand (kara) of a king, or the trunk (kara) of an elefant, the king being addressed here in both aspects (rājakuñjara, 'king-elefant').

[57] Read śūreṣu for sūreṣu.

[58] This is, again, a kind of pratyekabodhi.

[59] hayapriyāḥ = yavāḥ, according to the gloss (only in Lexicografers). But the word plays with another meaning, namely, 'fond of horses'.

grains[60] is not crushed' (166). 'No lie it is, he is surely 'Rice' (Śāli), crest-jewel of noble grains, for whose grains of virtue the king-parrots yearn forsooth' (167). The king, in this way, realizes that Śāli, as the impersonation of the Jina, has unexpectedly served him also for a noble purpose. Bhadrā then entertains the king sumptuously, and showers gifts upon him; the king returns to his palace (172).

iti Śālibhadrakathāyāṁ Śrīśreṇikāgamanavarṇano nāma caturthaḥ prakramaḥ.

Fifth Prakrama: Śālibhadra decides to turn ascetic, after debating the matter with his mother. His brother-in-law anticipates his course.

The fifth chapter announces its theme: 'The row of "Rice's" virtue-grains, can it in any way be counted? Yet the greatness of its measure must be divulged.'[61] 'The bliss of mortals and immortals, the rivers Gaṅgā and Sindhu[62], become tasteless in the overflowing ocean of Śāli's vāirāgya (loss of taste for the world), produced by the mere sight of the king'. As an elefant-keeper stains a scent-elefant[63], so the king stains him with the vermillion of passionlessness. A Bṛhaspati in discernment, he considers the secret of contending against the Demon Illusion. The existence of kings has brought him bliss (thru pratyekabodhi); his spiritual eye is clear as a star (7). Nevertheless (remembering how he had attracted the king) he rails at the 'royal serpent'[64], who constantly seeks to devour the unwary serpent-folk[65], and decides to resort to the mantra (sacred formula) and the divinity which will prevent the destruction of bliss by the 'king-disease'[66] (14). In this frame of mind he

---

[60] Read sarvasasyeṣu for sarvaśasyeṣu.

[61] śāleḥ puṇyakaṇaśreṇiḥ kiṁ gaṇeyā kathaṁcana, idamīyaḥ paraṁ mānamahimā paribhāvyatām.

[62] Gaṅgā in heaven where live the immortals; Sindhu upon earth where mortals live.

[63] Elefant during rut.

[64] rājasarpa; double entente, 'royal serpent', and 'anaconda'.

[65] bhogi-loka: double entente, 'serpent-folk', and 'folk devoted to the senses'.

[66] rājamandya: double entente, 'king as cause of disease', and = kṣaya-

resorts to the Gaṇa-leader (Sūri) Dharmaghoṣa[67], instructor in war against the 'Serpent Existence', who teaches him in a largish sermon how to cast off the fetters that bind to the world, by abandoning the triad of sins, and adopting the three restraints (gupti). Lauded by the three potencies, bhūs, bhuvas, and svar, he will then become 'Lord of the World' (35). Śāli, in ecstasy, cries out, 'I will abandon existence, and, thru your teaching, apply my mind to Salvation'. He then promises to return, as soon as he has bid farewell to his tenderhearted, loving mother (37).

Returning to the city he seats himself upon the roof of his palace, and lets his body hold communion with his mind. Like a good servant, his body promises obedience in the great undertaking before him: 'Then may I (the Body), bravely enduring hardships, stoutly bearing the burden imposed upon me, swift to obey thy (the Mind's) orders, not plunging into disrepute—may I, as thy servant, thus strive to fulfil thy every intention, so that (thou) my Master, after having obtained control, shalt not fail of thy purpose.'[68] Grasping now this connection of the Mind with its vehicle, the Body, Śāli regards existence as a victorious race, run by a horse in one day (āśvīna), coming to an end to-day or to-morrow (adyaśvīna; 46).

He meets his mother, and tells her that he has heard from the mouth of the Guru the Law that furnishes refuge, and that he is exceedingly pleased with it. A mother should feel honored by a son whose numberless virtues confer honor upon the family[69] (54). Bhadrā is much rejoiced, yet points out that the son of his father (Gobhadra) is not the bond-servant of lust, even tho he is sunk in the delights of Fortune (Śrī); the Jaina truth sits upon him as does the milk of a lioness upon a golden dish[70].

---

roga or rājayakṣma, 'consumption'.

[67] 'Sounder of the Law', frequently mentioned on similar occasions; e. g., Ratnacūḍa, p. 164 of Hertel's Translation; Hemavijaya's Kathāratnākara, story 177; Suali in his analysis of the Ādīśvara Caritra, p. 13, in *Studi Italiani di Filologia Indo-Iranica*, vol. 7 (1908).

[68] In this stanza the author employs the four reduplicated participial adjectives sāsahi, vāvahi, cācali, pāpati in the order in which they occur in Pāṇini; see Appendix iv.

[69] With conventional pun upon guṇa and vaṅśa.

[70] Proverbial, see Appendix i.

Enough for him, therefore, that he devote himself to a pious house-holder's life (gṛhidharma): let him practise to perfection (samyaktva) the twelve vows of laymen (60).

But Śāli soon disabuses her mind as to his intentions: 'Thou didst, O Mother, fitly say a faultless word, "Thou (Śāli) art the son of that father (Gobhadra)". Now ponder the significance of that statement' (63). 'Leaving out of question the possible superiority of children over parents, how can I be the son of an imperial Sage, and yet be devoted to the five senses?' (64). 'If thru thee, tho thou art but a single mother, I am thus happy here, what then is to be said of good conduct in which the eight good Mothers[71] are involved?' (65). 'With me as a son, being the earth-sustaining boar (Viṣṇu Avatar), having the form of Puruṣottama, be thou, O mother, like the primordial she-boar,[72] blessed in thy son' (66). In several other stanzas Śāli argues that the ascetic state will redound to the glory of both himself and his mother. 'The difference between a Sādhu (monk) and a Śrāvaka (lay-disciple) is said to be like that between Mount Meru and a mustard-seed; how can I then, O Mother, become an adept (siddhārtha)[73] while living the life of a house-holder'? (67). 'O Mother, do not therefore delay (thy permission)! Be thou the mother of a hero, a campaka-wreath among flower-garlands!' (69).

Bhadrā, struck by these words, as if by a hurricane, rolls in a swoon upon the stool of the earth, like a creeper cut from its root. No sooner is she restored than she resorts to every argument dictated by her love and Śāli's advantage, to induce him not to abandon her so early in life. Her love clings to him as a creeper to a tree; without him she is bereft of support; she is a heaven full of constellations, yet without sheen. Resignation does not suit early youth (76). She pleads quaintly: 'My child, like a verb-root that has two voices (parasmāipada and ātmanepada), thou enjoyest the bliss of both mortals and immortals; therefore it befits thee to occupy the two stations (padadvayī) of this world and the next world' (78). Then,

---

The eight sacred writings. Gloss, aṣṭāu pravacanamātaraḥ; cf. 1.37.

[72] ādipotriṇī = ādivarāhī.

[73] Pun on the meaning, 'white mustard'.

following another line, Bhadrā points out that Śāli's father had not taken the vow before he had adorned the family mountain with a young lion (namely, Śāli); that, therefore, Śāli also should first produce a son; afterwards he might place, as a coping, upon the temple of practical piety the five great vows (of a yati). For the present it is not fit that he should turn away (vāirāgya) from a world full of heavenly pleasures (90).

The son of Gobhadra (Gāubhadri) replies that his mother is preaching earthly, rather than heavenly interests; as for himself, he is sated with pleasure, because the praṇava (om) is established for him, embracing the knowledge (veda) which causes to spring up aversion to the world (99).

Returning to his evil experience with the king he bitterly exclaims: 'That influence which is spat out (left behind) by licentious king-demons must be avoided like eating by night' [74] (104). Further stanzas in the same strain contrast the call of the Lord Vīra to a holy life, which sits like a diadem upon the head, with the king's command which had suddenly fallen upon Śāli to his injury and sorrow: 'The crow, "possession by the king", making noise on high, surely bodes misfortune as it touches my head' (112). This is followed by four proverbs (115–118) which show how sensitive to treatment are noble things as contrasted with ignoble ones; e. g., 'A common garment is cleansed by pounding it with alcali-stones; a garment of the gods, on the other hand, is spoiled by the mere touch of man' (117). Thus the son of Gobhadra regards the king's favors as degradation, whereas others would delight in being his slaves: his soul and body are alike afflicted by him (122).

Bhadrā, in great grief, takes up this same idea: the king (rājan) has turned out to be the king-disease (rājamandya); she has performed a grievous ajākṛpaṇīya [75] act in introducing to him her son who is now afflicted by the king's breath. Nevertheless, she continues to argue the trials of ascetic life; the needs of her widowhood; the loveliness of his wives; his own charming youth; and the god-like career of sensuous pleasure open to him. Śāli finally yields to his mother's eloquence to the extent

---

[74] A sin with the Jainas. The niśābhojanavirati, 'abstention from eating by night', is described and illustrated in Vasupūjya Carita 1.412–567.

[75] See Appendix iv.

of abandoning one wife at a time, each day, so that it would take him 32 days to dispose of the lot (140).

Now there lives in that same city Subhadrā, a younger sister of Śāli, married to an excellent, virtuous husband, Dhanya by name. One day while Dhanya is bathing, tears drop from his wife's eyes upon his shoulder. Asked for the reason, she says that she is grieved because her brother, in order to restrain his senses, is daily giving up, one by one, his beloved wives. Dhanya replies that such cowardly conduct does not ferry one across the sea of desires; if procrastination in love and business[76] be ruinous, how much more speedy should be progress in religion? (151). Dhanya's seven other wives, taking Subhadrā's (and, incidentally, Śāli's) part, then ask him why he himself is not practising what he is preaching: 'Even cowards, more's the pity, can tell all about battles, but they scarcely breathe when strife roars its strident sounds' (153). Dhanya exclaims joyously that they, his wives, have become his spiritual guides; he will wait upon the Jina Lord to learn the holy life of an ascetic. As is usual in these cases, the wives make a show of objecting to being left without male support, and propose to follow him into homelessness. Dhanya is rejoiced, praises his wives, and meditates upon the arrival of the Lord Vīra (166).

iti śrīśālibhadralīlākathāyāṁ pañcamaḥ prastāvaḥ (! here, instead of prakramaḥ).

Sixth Prakrama: Śāli turns monk; his wanderings; his return home; and his pāraṇa by his mother in the preceding birth.

In the meantime the Lord Vīra, string of pearls of the triad bhūs, bhuvas, and svar, guide across the waters of existence, attended by Suras, who prepared his samavasaraṇa[77], arrives on the Vāibhāra mountain. His arrival is opportunely coincident with the faith that has come to Śālibhadra. Dhanya, who knows Vīra, the Cakravartin (Emperor) of the Holy Law, goes in company with his wives to the feet of the Lord, in order to obtain from him the means of salvation (8). Śāli then points out reproachfully to his mother Bhadrā, that his sister (Subhadrā)

[76] Two items of the puruṣārtha; see page 270, note 35.

[77] Place of descent from heaven, a technical Jaina term.

and her husband (Dhanya) have assumed leadership in heroic conduct: why may he not follow them? (11). Bhadrā, realizing at last that Śāli can not be swerved from his purpose, tells king Śreṇika that her son desired to take vows with the Saint Vīra, and asks him for the royal insignia,—golden pot, diadem, umbrella, and chowries,—in order to institute for her son the great festival of consecration (dīkṣā). The king, at first, questions whether Śāli will be able to endure the hardships of ascetic life, but, finally realizing Śāli's noble purpose, promises to arrange himself his ceremony of niṣkramaṇa[78]. He dismisses Bhadrā in a state of delight (22).

Śāli asks his father, the Sura Gobhadra, by whose grace, he knows, he has so far tasted the sensual bliss that belongs to the gods, to favor him still farther by making his earthly bliss bear fruit in the solemn act of 'going out'. He then enjoins upon his wives the care of his mother (35). After 'hero-flags' have been placed upon the cāitya sanctuaries, Śāli proceeds to the bath pavillion, where divine maidens pour over him the water of consecration; perfume and adorn him; and perform many other festive and sacramental acts in which the king's insignia play a part (50). Thereupon he proceeds in the company of the king, his mother, and his wives to the place of Vīra's samavasaraṇa, and reverently asks the Lord of the World to guide him to the religion that brings nirvāṇa. He puts on the monk's robe (paricīvaritaḥ); plucks out his hair[79], which Bhadrā gathers up together with his jewels; and is given by Holy Vīra himself the rank of a wandering ascetic (57).

Dhanya, his brother-in-law, with Subhadrā his wife (Śāli's sister), follows him into homelessness. The king returns to Rājagṛha. Bhadrā and Śāli's wives also go back sadly to a home which now seems like a divine grove without devadru trees, like heaven without the sun, like the firmament without the moon, like a country without king (64). The wives feel like an army abandoned by its leader, like duties performed without knowledge, like magic rites, ineffective because done without a spell, like a catena of virtue without good fortune, like she-elefants without the lord of the herd, like a threshing-floor without grain. They

---

78 See above, p. 271.

79 See my 'Life of Pārśvanātha', p. 115, note.

reproach themselves for not having followed him on the road to heaven, as stars follow the moon at the moment of his eclipse (73).

Dhanya and Śāli learn the scriptures from the mouth of the Saint Gāutama[80], and then enter upon a course of severe asceticism whose rigors in every particular of life, such as food, clothes, and bed, are effectively contrasted with the Sages' former life of luxury (99). They engage in fasts of one, two, three, and four months respectively, in consequence of which their figures become lean and emaciated. They revere many Jaina ikons, and practise severe forms of asceticism, actuated thruout by their longing for perfection. Freed from all earthly attachments, they move without haste upon the mendicant's path. In the end they are so emaciated that their skeletons rattle in their bodies. In the company of the Lord Vīra, and endowed with the (five) samitis[81], they arrive at the end of twelve years at the city of Rājagṛha (112). The Lord Vīra makes his samavasaraṇa upon Mount Vāibhāra, and is there revered by the people. As the two Munis are about to break a month's fast, they consult the Jina Lord, who advises them to let Śāli's mother perform this pious act (120). Unperceived by their former friends, they quickly go to Bhadrā's palace (126), and stand in the customary place of mendicants, emaciated, silent, emotionless (138).

Bhadrā is rejoiced at the arrival of her daughter (Subhadrā), her son (Śāli), her son-in-law (Dhanya), and the holy Lord Vīra, and communicates the event to Śāli's wives. She glories especially in the presence of Vīra and Śālibhadra, the latter being her sole possession, the life of her life (143). She contrasts her own fate, during the twelve years she has been left behind, with that of her daughter Subhadrā. Tho already overcome by old age, she had remained behind like a blind she-jackal, while her daughter, tender-limbed as a śirīṣa-blossom, had followed her husband Dhanya into homelessness, thus becoming the crest of the Meru-mountain of virtue. Dhanya her son-in-law, too, appears to her in the light of a great Muni: he shines with his

---

[80] Gāutama is the first disciple of Mahāvīra; see, e. g., Ayāraṅga Sutta 2.15–28.

[81] Five rules of personal behavior; see Umāsvāti's Tattvārthādhigama Sūtra 9.5

eight wives, who are like the embodied Mūrtis[82] (152). She calls upon her daughters-in-law, whose husband has returned upon a great ship from a distant country, as it were, to make preparations for the bodily comfort of the guests. This they joyously hasten to do, giving orders to the servants, who skip about nimbly and egg each other on[83] (161).

But Mother Bhadrā is not destined to break her son's fast. In spite of her longing to do honor and to entertain, she is so overcome by her emotions, that, as tho her eyes were shut, she does not see her son. Confused by the flood of her thoughts, she does not show honor to the two Munis as they stand in the court of the house (169). Śāli's wives also regret their separation from him, blaming themselves because they have not followed him into homelessness. When they turn their sight upon him, they, too, are unable to see him for the tears in their eyes; and he, in turn, is so emaciated as to be unrecognizable (179).

The sages' equanimity is not at all disturbed by this apparent disregard of their needs (186). As they are about to pass out of the city, a certain Mathitahārikā[84], a middle-aged woman (kātyāyanī), sees Śāli and is filled with great joy and exaltation, 'as tho she were a mermaid (jalamānuṣī) in the milk-ocean of delight'. She sheds tears of joy, and milk oozes from her breasts, as tho in the stress of motherhood. Poor as she is, she offers sour milk as alms. The two Sādhus, having accepted the alms, 'purified by every test (sarvopadhāśuddha),' depart (204). Śāli asks Holy Vīra how his pāraṇa came about, and the Master tells him that the woman, in her former birth, was his mother Dhanyā, dwelling in Śāligrāma, and that she had now become a noble woman (satyā) thru her gift of sour milk (207).

iti śrīśālilīlākathāyāṁ śrīśālibhadravihāramātṛgṛhāgamanapāraṇavarṇano nāma ṣaṣṭhaḥ prastāvaḥ.

Seventh Prakrama: Śālibhadra and Dhanya, ultimately enlightened, die by fast, and attain to Supreme Bliss.

Śāli, remembering Holy Vīra's sayings, ponders the course of his own life. To begin with, man in general skips about as an

[82] The gloss lists these Mūrtis, to wit: kṣiti, jala, pavana, hutāśana, yajamāna, ākāśa, candra, and sūrya.

[83] chireyāhirāṁ cakrur nṛtyanto 'tyantacañcalāḥ; see Appendix ii.

[84] This is either a proper noun, or means 'with her necklace disarranged'.

actor in the play of Existence[85]. He next lists and contrasts the events of his present life with those of his pre-birth: his life in a noble city, with his former life in a low-caste village; his mother's gift of the precious shawls to her daughters-in-law, with his former mother's destitution. In his former birth he did not even know the name of his father, much less had he seen him in the flesh; in his present birth his father Gobhadra (after he had become a god) had given the chireyāhirā-command[86] here on earth in his behalf (7). And so he refers everything back to the time when, in his former birth, his mother Dhanyā procured the ingredients for a feast from her compassionate neighbors, enabling him to gratify the Muni with the food he himself so keenly desired. But for the Muni's arrival, his birth as a villager would have been fruitless. And all led up to his receiving his pāraṇa from the hands of his former mother (15). Reflecting thus, as on the om of the Veda 'Aversion from the World', he turns to his brother-Muni, Dhanya, who is traveling on the way to the fortress 'Excellent'; reminds him of his early leadership when he himself (Śāli) was still weak in the flesh; and bids him engage together with himself in the final battle of victory over the Chief Trickster, 'Illusion'[87]. Dhanya responds enthusiastically, pointing out, in harmony with his character, that delay or hesitancy pierce the vitals (of purpose) like an arrow, and that Śāli, in the past, had not made a long story of it, when there was question of giving alms (dāna). They go to Holy Vīra, prostrate themselves before him, and constitute him their flag on the top of the high palace 'Self-restraint' (29). Vīra encourages them to shoot with unerring aim at the target 'Contemplation' (dhyāna). They adopt the (five) Rules of Conduct (samiti), and abandon the four kinds of food along with all desires and hopes. Sustained in their resolution by the Sage Gāutama, they await death from starvation under a tree[88] (38).

Bhadrā and her daughters-in-law, all clad in white robes, their faces veiled, go out to do honor to the Jina (Vīra). They are joined by King Śreṇika and his son and minister, Abhayakumā-

---

[85] narīnartti naṭaḥ prāṇī kaṭare bhavanāṭake. For kaṭare see Appendix ii.

[86] See Appendix ii.

[87] dhūrtarājaṁ mahāmoham.

[88] pādapopagamaṁ nāmānaśanam; see Appendix iii.

ra. When Bhadrā fails to see Śāli and Dhanya with the Lord, she asks about them, and he tells her that they are engaged in the pīdapopagama on the Vāibhāra mount (55). Bhadrā, like a haṅsa-bird in a cage, like a jhaṣī-fish caught in a net, like a she-antelope struck by an arrow, terribly disturbed in mind, sighing, stumbling, and falling down at every step, wailing pitifully, approaches the place where are the two Munis. She is followed by Śreṇika and Abhayakumāra. When she sees them lying on the mountain-top, as tho they had been struck by lightning, she and her retinue fall into a swoon (61). After being revived, she bewails long and bitterly her fate as wife and mother. She is a woman who had one child and many cares. Her crowning misery is, that she could not retain her child for life, at the time when he returned home to break a month's fast. She did not then appraise her Muni son at his full value (76). She also neglected Dhanya, her son-in-law, who, instead of being Śāli's play-fellow, became his guide in spiritual matters (83). Now she adresses Śāli as an accomplished Arhat, as river of equanimity, as one to whom good and evil are the same, as one to whom a (burning) sword and (cool) sandal are the same [89]. She begs him to give answer, or to favor her, if only with a look (95). Śāli's wives join Bhadrā in regrets over their abandonment of their husband: 'weighed in the gold-scale of love, they are discovered to be equal to the (slight weight of a) guñjā [90]' (100). It will redound to their everlasting shame that their husband, standing in the courtyard (of Bhadrā's house), did not regard them even with a look (105). They beg him to return, but, if he is resolved to fast to death, let him at least present them with the ambrosia of his speech. Bhadrā is moved by their laments to the pitch of again falling into a faint, and, after being restored, continues to cry (112).

At this point King Śreṇika steps into the breach, by consoling her with the thought that she is going to be counted most honorable and praiseworthy among noble women; that her son will be honored even by the gods; and that, of all women, she will wear a diadem upon her brow for having given birth to a lion-

[89] vāsīcandanakalpa; see Appendix iii.

[90] A berry used as a small weight; see the note on p. 61 of Tawney's Translation of Prabandhacintāmaṇi.

son who roars at the 'Elefant Delusion'. Let her, therefore, with resolute words encourage her son in his great struggle (112). Bhadrā takes his words to heart; gives over her grief; consoles her daughters-in-law; encourages her heroic son to victory; glories in her own and her daughters-in-law's distinction; blesses the hard road to perfection (siddhi) which the two Munis are treading; and returns to the city (131). Śāli and Dhanya ride under the sailorship of their captain Gāutama upon the ship 'Asceticism' (saṁnyāsa), die, and are reborn as supreme gods in the Heaven called Sarvārthasiddha where they enjoy the highest bliss (145).

iti śrīśālibhadracarite sarvārthasiddhiprāptivarṇano nāma saptamaḥ prakramaḥ.

APPENDICES

Appendix i: Proverbs and Proverbial Expressions

Like most Jaina fiction texts, and, indeed, like most fiction texts in general, the author or redactor of the Śālibhadra Carita interlards his rather slender story with proverbs or proverbial expressions. Some of these occur elsewhere, but the majority appear to be new. The Jaina texts are not only full of religious apothegms (dharma), but they also exploit every fase of wordly wisdom (nīti, artha, kāuṭilya). To some extent such sayings are, doubtless, original with the Jaina writers, but, no less certainly, the same writers draw from the springs of popular inspiration in this respect, no less than in respect of narrative and folk-lore. These nīti-stanzas will have to be gathered and sifted into a huge supplement to Böhtlingk's *Indische Sprüche*, so deservedly famous in Indic filology[1]. For the present a few illustrations of these conditions shall suffice. Thus:

1.25ab: uttamāḥ svaguṇāiḥ khyātā madhyamās tu pitur guṇāiḥ.

'Highest is the character of them that are famous thru their own virtue; middling the character of them that are famous thru their father's virtue' (Böhtlingk, 1178, 1182).

---

[1] How familiar among the Jainas these stanzas are may be gathered conveniently from the foot-notes to Tawney's Translation of Prabandhacintāmaṇi, pp. 20, 23, 32, 35, 40, 68, 78, 92, 114, 138, 182, 198. See also my 'Life of Pārśvanātha', pp. 208 ff.

3.34: siṁhārkanṛpadeveṣu bāla ity avahīlanā,
gūḍhaprāuḍhapratāpeṣu [2] viduṣāṁ nahi yujyate.

'It is not proper for wise people to underestimate lions, the sun, a prince, or a god on account of their youth, because great power is hidden in these' (Böhtlingk, 7043, with avahīlanā, not avahelanā [3], as Bö. emends).

4.126: parakāvyaiḥ kavitvaṁ yad garvo yācitabhūṣaṇāiḥ,
yā ca yācanayā tṛptis tad etan mūrkhalakṣaṇam.

'When people establish for themselves the reputation of being poets thru others' poetry, or when they are proud of borrowed jewels, or satisfy their hunger thru begging—all that is the mark of a fool' (cf. Böhtlingk, 3917).

5.9: nṛsiṅhā na samīhante bhakṣyaṁ kakṣīkṛtaṁ parāiḥ,
svīkurvanti tu goṣṭhaśvās tat kṛtvā vigrahāgraham.

'Man-lions do not desire the food tucked away in the hem of others' garments [4]; stable-dogs appropriate that, making it an occasion for strife.' Cf. Böhtlingk, 4979, 7322; Bhāvadevasūri's Pārśvanātha Caritra 5.182.

1.48, describing widowhood:
nimnaṁ strījanma tatrāpi vāidhavyaṁ navyaduḥkhakṛt,
dāusthyaṁ (!) sthānam anāsthāyā dāsyaṁ hāsyakaraṁ jane.

'Low-grade is the birth of a woman. Her widowhood produces new pain. An evil station is that in which there is no support; servitude is cause for derision with people.'

3.29–30, describing men's and women's relation to the upkeep of a family:

stambhaḥ sāudhaṁ na tu sthūṇā yūthaṁ hastī na hastinī,
durālānaṁ latā nāiva rathamukṣā na gāur yathā,
evam uccāiḥ kulābhāraṁ sāttvikaḥ puruṣo 'rhati,
abalā nāmadhāmabhyāṁ na nārī kovidāpy aho.

'The (male) stambha-post is (the foundation of) the palace, not the (female) sthūṇā-pillar [5]; the male elefant is the herd, not the she-elefant. The (female) creeper is not at all a hard

---

[2] Variant reading, gūḍhaprāuḍhaprabhāveṣu.

[3] Both Sanskrit words seem to me back-formations from Prākritic forms (avahīrei) which are ultimately derived from Skt. avadhīraya-, 'despise'.

[4] The conventional Hindu pocket.

[5] The noun stambha is masculine in gender; sthūṇā is feminine.

fetter (for an elefant to break); the cow is not a draught-ox[6]. Thus a noble man is fit to hold high the family; not, alas! a woman, weak by name and character, even tho she be an intelligent woman'.

3.58, dealing with the duty of son to father:

janakaṁ svaṁ kalāvantaṁ budhaḥ saṁnihitaḥ sutaḥ,
trāyate vatsa no sūram api mandas tamograhāt.

The stanza has two meanings: 'A wise son (the planet Mercury) protects his accomplished father (the moon with its fases) when stationed near him, O Child; but not a foolish one (the planet Saturn) even a learned one (the Sun) from misfortune (eclipse)'.

3.89–93, describe a father's love for his son.

4.36 ff., describe the relation between wives and mothers-in-law.

5.98, illustrates equanimity.

5.105, showing that subservience is a kill-joy:

parājñā bhogasāukhyeṣu sarvāñgasubhageṣv api,
trasarekheva[7] ratneṣu mahāmahimahānaye.

'The command of another reduces pleasures, even tho they delight in every (other) particular, just as a floating line in jewels reduces their value.'

5.115–118: objects of high quality are easily spoiled by contact with coarse persons or things.

5.116: suvarṇaṁ vahninikṣiptaṁ varṇikāvṛddhim aśnute,
uṣṇāśvāsābhiyoge 'pi māuktikaṁ mlānam īyate.

'Gold thrown into fire is improved in quality, but a pearl touched even by warm breath loses its lustre.'

5.117: sāmānyavasanaṁ kṣāraśilākuṭṭakakuṭṭanāiḥ
dīpyate, devadūṣyaṁ tu narasparśena dūṣyate.

'Garments of average people are made to shine by pounding them with alcali stones; but the garments of the gods are defiled by the touch of man.'

5.153: kātarā api saṁgrāmāvartām āvartayanty aho,
na śvasanty api nisvānodvāmasāṁrāviṇe raṇe.

---

[6] For rathamukṣā, see p. 301 and note 12[a].

[7] For trasa-rekhā, see p. 304.

'Behold, even cowards tell tales of battle; but they do not even breathe when battle resounds with its strident roar.'[7a]

The following are examples of proverbial expressions which accompany, *pari passu*, the set proverb stanzas, both constant elements of fiction:

1.44[cd]: vadanti prati putraṁ hi pratyanīkaṁ na mātaraḥ,
'Mothers do not contradict their sons.'

3.44: mahānto hi jātu muñcanti nāucitīm,
'Noble men do not neglect decorum.'

5.57: siṅhīpayaḥ svarṇapātra evāvatiṣṭhate,
'The milk of a lioness remains only in a golden vessel.'

This is supported in the gloss by a nīti-śloka which does not occur in Böhtlingk:

kṣīraṁ śvānodare siṅhīdugdham asvarṇabhājane,
niṣpuṇye śrī rasendro 'gnāu dharmas tiṣṭhati nādhame.

'Milk does not remain in the belly of a dog; the milk of a lioness in a dish which is not gold; Fortune in him that has not accumulated a stock of merit; quicksilver in the fire; or religion in the vile.'

6.2: mahatām.....spṛhāprāptī yugmajāte iva dhruvam,
'Unfailingly desire and fulfilment, as tho they were twins, come to noble (pious) men.'

Appendix ii: Characteristic Jaina Words and Forms.

Regarding the following, I do not guarantee that each item is exclusively Jaina. Each word or form occurs more or less habitually in Jaina literature, presumably mostly in literature composed in Guzerat. They are part of a larger collection of peculiarities, some of which may be gathered from the word-lists printed on pp. 220 ff. of my 'Life and Stories of the Jaina Savior Pārśvanātha' (Baltimore, 1919), and from the prefaces and introductions to the texts or translations of other Jaina fiction texts, such as Hemacandra's Pariśiṣṭaparvan; Pradyumnācārya's Samarādityasaṁkṣepa; the Kathākośa; Merutuñga's Prabandhacintāmaṇi; Jinakīrti's Pālagopālakathānakam; the

7a nisvāna-udvāma-saṁrāviṇe: "characterised by uproar caused by emission (udvāma; not recorded in Lexx.) of shouts"??

Bharaṭakadvātriṅśikā; the Pañcadaṇḍachattraprabandha, and others. A larger collection of such material will be found in the author's forthcoming paper, 'On some Aspects of Jaina Sanskrit', which will show that this language has retained a certain productivity not altogether dependent upon Prākritic or geografical and dialectal influences.

Śālibhadra's list may be fitly headed by a group of interjections which contain the elements re and ari (are), used mostly to address inferiors, in the sense of 'sirrah' or to express wonder:

kaṭare in 1.88; 2. 58; 7.3, 'wonderful to narrate', glossed by āścaryabhūtam in 2. 58; by āścaryārthe in 7. 3. At 1. 88 in parallelism with aho, and arire (see next). This word occurs also in Bhāvadevasūri's Pārśvanātha 3. 492; 8.48, glossed, adbhutārtham avyayam, 'an indeclinable, expressing wonder'; in Hemacandrasūriprabandha, śloka 63 (Edition of the Prabhāvaka Carita, p. 300), kaṭare jananībhaktir uttamānāṁ kaṣopalaḥ, 'behold, devotion to one's mother is the touchstone of noble men.' In Kathākośa, in a stanza printed in Tawney's Translation, p. 234, in a note to p. 3, lines 25–28, kaṭare karma-lāghavam, 'strange to tell, my karma is light!' Pischel, *Hemacandra's Grammatik der Prākritsprachen*, vol. i, p. 157 (anent 4.350), prints a doubtful and unexplained word kaṭari, which is the Apabhraṅśa form, and perhaps Prākrit form in general. Of this he cites a variant kūṭare, in vol. ii, p. 187. This, presumably, is the same word. In the Apabhraṅśa Sanatkumāracaritam, elaborated by Jacobi, in the Abhandlungen der Bayerischen Akademie der Wissenschaften, München 1921, kaṭari occurs in stanza 777 by the side of vapuri and ari, in a sense similar to our word. In the Index, s. v. kaṭari, Jacobi also mentions kaṭa, and kata kaṭa, as occurring in the Neminähacariu (Neminăthacarita), of which his Sanatkumāra Edition is a part. The Apabhraṅśa vapuri is a combination of vapus, which even in the RV. means 'marvel', and ri. The meaning is again āścaryam.

arire, in connection with aho and kaṭare, also something like 'wonderful to tell'. The word is probably Jaina only, perhaps of Apabhraṅśa origin; see ari are, ari ari, ari ri, and arire in the Index to Sanatkumāracarita, Jacobi, l. c., Glossary, p. 106. Sanskrit lexicografers report arare and areare. Mallinātha Caritra 1.130, 264; 2. 378 has are re.

The exclamation ehi re yāhi re, 'come here sirrah, go sirrah!', yields the pretty feminine adjective ehireyāhirā with kriyā, 'work', expressed or understood. Thus in 6.161, ehireyāhirāṁ cakruḥ, 'they ordered about'; and in 7.7, ehireyāhirākāri, 'a great ordering about was caused'. In Pārśvanātha 6.82, karoti bhavakūpe 'sminn ehireyāhirāṁ kriyām, 'he makes in the puddle of this existence a great ordering about (sc., a great stir, or a great pother)'. The gloss there is, ehi re! yāhi re! yasyāṁ kriyāyāṁ sā ehireyāhirā, tām. The word is listed in the Gaṇa mayūravyaṅsakādi (to Pāṇini 2.1.72), but is not quotable in non-Jaina Sanskrit literature,. It may, therefore, have been taken by the Jainas from Grammar. See below, p. 306 ff.

Other words that recur in Jaina writers are:

nīrañgī, 'veil', in nīrangī-channa-vadanāḥ, 7.46, glossed kāusumbhavastram, tena channaṁ ḍhañkitaṁ vadanaṁ yāsāṁ tāḥ (ḍhañkitam, not in Lexs.). This word occurs also in Mallinātha Caritra 3.68; Pariśiṣṭaparvan 2.8, 149, 496; Bharaṭakadvātriṅśikā 3; and in Samarād. 4.555. It is listed in Hemacandra's Deśīnāmamālā 2.20, 90; 4.31, in the forms ṇiraṁgī and ṇīraṁgī (glossed nīrañgikā). Tawney, Translation of Kathākośa, p. xxiii, quotes nīrañgī as a Prākrit word. In Pārśvanātha, 8.185, the word occurs in the feminine compound kṛtanīrañgikā.

śrīkarī, 'palanquin', 5.118; 6.45; Pārśvanātha 6.514 (glossed, sukhāsanam); Uttamacaritrakathānaka 234.

rora, 'laborer, or 'beggar', in rora-gṛha, 1.91. Pariśiṣṭaparvan 8.72, 291, and Mallinātha Caritra 7. 19 have the same word in the same sense. Pārśvanātha 8.221 has rāurageha, 'house of a laborer'. The form rora occurs also in the Aghata tale; see Charlotte Krause, *Prinz Aghata* (Leipzig, 1922), pp. 148, note 2; 150, note 1; it there alternates with rañka, 'beggar', which, according to Hertel, in his edition of Bharaṭakadvātriṅśikā, p. 54^{b}, is of Gujarātī origin. But the word occurs also outside that sfere. Deśīnāmamālā 7.11 has rora, along with roghasa and roṁkaṇa, all in the sense of rañka. Rora in the same sense in Dhanapāla's Pāiyalacchi, stanza 35, with many synonyms for 'poor'.

maṣī-bheda, in maṣībhedam akurvāṇaḥ, 3.71. Glossed, dānādicāuryam asatyaṁ ca maṣībhedaḥ. The expression maṣībhedam akurvāṇah, therefore, seems to mean, 'not making an infraction of good character'. The subject of akurvāṇaḥ is the pious merchant Gobhadra, Śālibhadra's father, who is praised as a holy man in a Prākrit śloka, reported above, p. 261. The statement there suits our word. In Pārśvanātha 6.410 there is a half-śloka, vināivādhyayanaṁ siddhir lebhe māṣatuṣādibhiḥ, where māṣatuṣādibhiḥ is glossed by muniviśeṣāiḥ, 'totally without study perfection (or, magic power) has been obtained by the Sages so designated'. There seems to be some connection between maṣībheda and māṣatuṣādayaḥ, māṣa being 'one who is of good character' (namely maṣī). The word tuṣa, in the same sense, is also unknown hitherto.

pheruṇḍa = pheraṇḍa, 6.95 (glossed by sṛgāla), Mallinātha Caritra 1.457, 'jackal'. So also Pārśvanātha 3.904, glossed the same way. Both forms in Lexs. Cf. phera, pheru, and pherava.

agañjita, 3.70, 'unterrified', also Pārśvanātha 6.376 (here glossed, abhīta). Dhātupāṭha has a root gañj, in the sense of garj, 'roar'.

maṅginī, 3.18, glossed nāuḥ, 'ship'. Also Pariśiṣṭaparvan 2. 402; Mallinātha Caritra 2.337.

cheka, 3.21, 46, here glossed, chekā vidvāṅsaḥ, 'wise', 'cunning'. Also Pariśiṣṭaparvan 2.447; Siṅhāsanadvātriṅśikā, pp. 295, 327 (Weber, Ind. Stud. xv).

ratha-kaṭyā, 2.16, glossed, rathānāṁ samūhaḥ, 'mass of wagons'. Also cited in Böhtlingk's Lexicon from some Pārśvanāthacarita, 4.172, which is not by Bhāvadevasūri. Lexicografers and Grammarians have ratha-kaḍyā.

puṣpadantāu, dual, 3.119, glossed, divākaraniśākarāu, 'sun and moon'. Also Śatruṁjayamāhātmya 14.225. Lexs. have puṣpavantāu in the same sense.

chaṭācchoṭa, 1.104; 4.89. The passages are as follows: 1.104, ānandāśrujalodgārāiś chaṭācchoṭaṁ kirann iva; 4.89, haricandana-kāśmīra-chaṭācchoṭa-dharā dharā. The compound chaṭācchoṭa seems to mean 'mass', in 4.89 'the earth carrying a mass of sandal and saffron trees'; cf. Prākrit chaḍā, 'mass', in Jacobi's *Ausgewählte Erzählungen*, p. 109^b (Skt. chaṭā). But in Pañcadaṇḍachattraprabandha, p. 24, we have: makara-maccha-nakracakra-suṅsumāra-gajaturagavṛṣabhākārapuccha-chaṭāchoṭotkalitaṁ nīranidhim, which Weber (p. 65) translates, 'das meer, das durch die schwanzschläge von makara, fischen, krokodil-schaaren, delphinen, und von elephanten-, rossen-, stieren-ähnlichen gestalten aufgepeitscht ward'. Weber, p. 24, note 112, cites Molesworth, *Mahratti Dictionary*; 'Mahratti and Gujarati chaṭāchoṭa, imitation of the sound of slashing or cutting rapidly a soft, yielding and rushing substance (as plantain-trees, hair, etc.)'. I find it impossible to harmonize the last statement with the use of the word in Śālibhadra.

jemana, 2.73, 'eating', in the combination, riṅṣaṇaṁ (for riñkhaṇaṁ 'crawling') kramaṇaṁ jemanam. Root jem also in Dharmaparīkṣā (see Mironow, p. 8, note 10). See Hemacandra, IV, 110, 230; and Jacobi, *Ausgewählte Erzählungen in Māhārāṣṭrī*, Vocabulary, s.vv. jimiya and jemei.

kad-āgraha, 'evil inclination', 1.43; Pārśvanātha 6.787.

caturthapuruṣārtha, 3.22; Mallinātha Caritra 3.208; Vasupūjya Carita 4.8 ff., 'fourth purpose of man', i. e., mokṣa, 'release'. The four puruṣārtha are: dharma, artha, kāma, and mokṣa. Śālibhadra 4.109 mentions a puruṣārtha-trayī, followed by the fourth, namely mokṣa. Mallinātha Caritra 2.232 puruṣārthas tṛtīyaḥ is a kenning for 'love'. Cf. Weber, *Die Griechen in Indien*, p. 30, for possible connection with Greek ideas.

akāṇakrīta-krayāṇaka, 4.7, glossed, dānacāuryarahitapaṇya [8], 'dealing in properly acquired goods': kāṇaka-krayin, 'purchaser of stolen goods', Bhāvadevasūri's Pārśvanātha Caritra 8.247. See Bloomfield, 'Life and Stories of the Jaina Savoir Pārśvanātha,' pp. 217, 234; and, 'The Art of Stealing in Hindu Fiction', *American Journal of Philology* 44.105.

sarvārthasiddha (sc. mahāvimāna), 'heaven of complete accomplishment': 7.139; Rāuhiṇeya Caritra 468; Mahāvira Carita 10.181.

The most important word nyuñchana, apparently exclusively Jaina, occurs twice in Śālibhadra, 1.42; 7.64. In the first passage the pious and proper shepherd boy Saṁgama asks his destitute mother to prepare for him a luxurious feast, quite beyond her means, and she replies, to wit:

mātā provāca he vatsa rūpanārāyaṇasya te,
nijalīlāvilāsasya bālakasya baliḥ kriye. 41.
nyuñchanaṁ tava netrāṇāṁ bhāṣitasyāvatāraṇam,
bhrāmye 'haṁ bhujayor jātamukhakasya mriye mriye. 42.

---

[8] From this it seems to follow that it was thought improper to sell things acquired by gift.

In 7.64 Bhadrā hears that her son Śālibhadra has gone to the Vāibhāra mountain to die by fast under a tree (pādapopagama), and she wails:

mriye mriye tavāsyasya nyuñchanaṁ tava netrayoḥ,
baliḥ kriye ca te yāmi nirmamatve 'vatāraṇam.

The comm. glosses avatāraṇam with lokoktyā "avataraṇum".

In Bhāvadevasūri's Pārśvanātha Caritra 6.1188 we have śironyuñchanaka, apparently in the sense of, 'some arrangement of the hair of the head':

pṛṣṭāu ca cakriṇā kiṁ bho ihāgamanakāraṇam,
kevalaṁ tāu dhunītaḥ sma śironyuñchanakaṁ kila.

'And when the Emperor (Sanatkumāra) asked the two (gods, Vijaya and Vāijayanta): "Why, Sirs, have you come here?", they merely shook their......'. This passage is wanting in the three versions of the Sanatkumāra conversion story, Kathākośa p. 35, middle; in the Māhārāṣṭrī version, Jacobi, *Ausgewählte Erzählungen*, p. 21, l. 5; and in the Apabhraṅśa version from the Neminähacariu, published by Jacobi in Abhandlungen der Bayerischen Akademie, 1921 (stanza 739, p. 58). The latter text, however, has the word niuṁchaṇauṁ in 777; see pp. 62, 128.

Rāuhiṇeya Caritra, stanza 122, describes the following ceremony which the mother of the thief Rāuhiṇeya undertakes in honor of his first theft:

nyuñchanāni vidhāyāśu pradīpaṁ saptavartibhiḥ,
vidhāya tilakaṁ mātā putrāyety āśiṣaṁ dadāu.

The root uñch, 'gather', 'glean'; nir-uñchana, 'lustration', and proñch, 'wipe out', throw no light on nyuñchana.

In 4.133 occurs Naggati as the name of one of the four Pratyekabuddhas, famous both in Buddhist and Jaina literature. This 'back-formation' of Prākrit Naggaï seems to be a genuine and exclusive product of Jaina Sanskrit writers, for it is employed also by Lakṣmīvallabha in his Dīpikā on the Naggaï story in Devendra's commentary on Uttarādhyayana Sūtra (Jacobi, *Ausgewählte Erzählungen*, pp. 48 ff.). The proper noun Nagnajit occurs as early as Mahābhārata (3.15257; 5.1882; 7.120); its Pāli form is Naggaji, Kumbhakāra Jātaka (408). Almost one would think that the avoidance by the Jaina Sanskrit writers of the form nagnajit, 'conquering the naked', is to spare the feelings of the Digambaras, who might not like its implication. But the form Naggati has no discernible association or meaning. In Śālibhadra 5.11 the word netra, 'kind of a cloth', is glossed by paṭṭakūlam, which occurs in the text of Rāuhiṇeya Caritra 147, 176, 313; in Bharaṭakadvātriṅśikā 3; and in 'Die Abenteuer Ambadas', by Charlotte Krause, *Indische Erzähler*, Band iv, p. 167. Hertel in his edition of Bhar., p. 53^b, derives the Sanskrit word from Old Gujarātī paṭakula, 'silk cloth', citing other forms from Hindu dialects.

The word su-dhī, 'teacher' (śrīdharmakumārasudhiyaḥ, 'spiritual teachers of Dh.') occurs at the head of the Editors' Introduction to Śālibhadra. It is quoted otherwise only from the Kośas, except that it is found in Prabandhacintāmaṇi, p. 2, where Tawney reads with some mss. svadhiyaḥ.

The 'root' vidhyāi, 'to go out', 'be extinguished', a Sanskrit back-formation of Pāli-Prākrit vijjhāi (itself from Sk. vi-kṣāi 'burn out') is common, eclectically, in some Jaina Sanskrit texts, and totally wanting in others. See my 'Life of Pārśvanātha', pp. 220 ff.[9] It does not occur in the text of Śālibhadra, which has opportunity to use it (nirvāpaya-, 'extinguish', in 3.82; 4.26; 7.113); but the gloss at 6.176 knows the word: jvalatkāṣṭhaṁ nīreṇa vidhāpyate (! for vidhyāpyate), 'a burning log is extinguished by water'.

Of grammatical peculiarities which Śālibhadra shares with other Jaina texts the most noteworthy is the desiderative participle cikīḥ 1.28; 4.113; 5.137 (glossed, cikīrṣati), 'desiring to perform', all times at the end of a compound. The word occurs also Pārśvanātha 8. 25 (glossed, kartum ichuḥ); Pariśiṣṭaparvan 7. 90; 8. 453; Mallinātha Caritra 3. 116, 117; Jinakīrti's Pālagopālakathānaka 123, 124, 177; Merutuṅga, Nabhākarāja Carita 7. 60; 22. 22; Uttamacaritrakathānaka, 1. 98; and in the tale of Aghata, elaborated by Charlotte Krause, *Prinz Aghata* (Leipzig, 1922), verse 204; cf. p. 148, note 2. The form is reported by Vopadeva, but is not quotable from any Brahmanical text (cf. Whitney, *Sanskrit Grammar* §392^d); there is, at present, no way of deciding whether or not the Jainas took and popularized the word from grammar merely.[10]

---

[9] Add, vidhyāpayitum 'to extinguish', Mallinātha Caritra 7.390.

[10] Mallinātha Caritra, 1.303, has cikīrṣu.

Śālibhadra 6.25; Mallinātha Caritra 7. 34, 917; and Pariśiṣṭaparvan 1.153 have the secondary pronominal adjective yāuṣmākīṇa, 'your', otherwise reported only by grammarians and lexicografers; Mallinātha 7. 677 has the corresponding āsmākīna (Pāṇini); cf. māmakīna and tāvakīna, Mallinātha 7. 124. Mākīna occurs a single time in RV. Śālibhadra 5.1 has idamīya, 'pertaining to him' (glossed, asyāyam), patterned after tadīya, etc., whereas Pārśvanātha 3.465 abandons tvadīya in favor of tvatya, glossed tvadīya (see Whitney, 1245^b). Cf. kvatya, 'whence', in Mahāvīra Carita 11.43 (also Pāṇini). The Prakritism imāiḥ for ebhiḥ occurs somewhere in Pariśiṣṭaparvan; in Pārśvanātha 1.805; 6.767; 7.398; and in Samarādityasaṁkṣepa 4.508, 619; 6.385; 8.520. It may be presumed that other analogical or Prākritic pronominal forms will turn up in Jaina Sanskrit.

In Śālibhadra 5.102 the duplication bhogā-bhoga is Pāli-Prākritic; see my 'Life of Pārśvanātha', p. 223. For the periphrastic perfect participle saṁbhāvayāmāsivān 5. 167, see ib. pp. 237 ff., where are cited parallels from Pārśvanātha and Samarādityasaṁkṣepa. In Mallinātha Caritra 7.993, occurs the fem. kathayāmāsuṣī. The imperfect third plural āiyaruḥ, 1.52; 4.4, is supported by the grammarians, but is not otherwise quotable; cf. the present third plural iyrati in Pārśvanātha, Pariśiṣṭaparvan; see ib., p. 237, and add Mallinātha Caritra 8. 63. Finally, the expression, with mixed syntax, yūyam abhūvan, 5.157, for bhavantyo 'bhūvan, is paralleled by tvam abhūt, for bhavān abhūt in Pañcadaṇḍachattraprabandha, p. 26, l. 9. In Śālibhadra 5.69 the expression, mātar mā tad vilambadhvam, 'Mother, do not therefore delay!', is based upon the same unconscious blend between mātar and the polite plural bhavatyaḥ.

Appendix iii: New words not in the Lexicons.

Considering that the Śālibhadra Carita is a small text it shows a rather surprising number of new words, aside from an even larger number which it shares with native lexicons and grammars; see below, pp. 306ff. They are not all of them of equal importance; some are morfological variants of familiar words; some pertain to Jaina dogmatics; and some are more or less obscure in meaning. Collectively they seem, however, to show, along with the considerable list of new words in Bhāvadevasūri's Pārśvanātha

Caritra[11], that the springs of Jainistic language have by no means run dry since the days of Hemacandra. The following list contains more than 100 more or less novel items of varying degrees of interest or originality:

1.29: maraṭṭa in the following śloka:

saṁmārjanaṁ cakārāryā harmyāṇāṁ karmaṇām iva
gharaṭṭāir dalayāmāsa maraṭṭāir vipadām iva.

Here the word maraṭṭāiḥ, glossed ahaṁkārāiḥ prakarṣāir vā, is not in the Lexs. 'The noble lady scrubbed houses, as one wipes off the effect of deeds (done in a previous existence); with grindstones, she rubbed off. . . .'

1.36: kukṣi-śambalin, glossed, pātheyam, 'one whose (only) provisions are in his belly', that is, 'one who takes no provisions with him'.

1.52: āveśin, in āveśinyas tayā śucā, 'affected' (by this grief). Gloss, tena śokena . . . vyākulāḥ.

1.57: iṣṭikāpākamūṣikā in the following śloka:

ājanmaduḥkhadagdhāṁ māṁ vidagdhā api mugdhavat |
tāpaṁ kiṁ pṛchata[12] svacchā iṣṭikāpākamūṣikām ||

'Why do ye tho ye are wise, foolish-like, plainly ask me, who have been afflicted (burned) by misfortune from the time of my birth, about my grief (fire), me who am (like) a mouse baked into a brick?' This translation of iṣṭikāpākamūṣikā is, of course, conjectural, my idea being, 'why do you ask a mouse baked into a brick whether it is hot'? Note that the verse is redolent of words for heat.

1.70: varārakṣas, sc. sneham, glossed, pradhānato rakṣaṇaṁ yasya taṁ sneham (pradhānarakṣaṇīyam). The word seems to mean, 'exercising especial care'.

1.82: saṁtoṣa-dṛk, in saṁtoṣa-dṛg-bhaya, glossed, dṛṣṭi-laganabhaya, seems to be eufemism for 'envious look', in the nature of 'evil eye'. Cf. Crooke, *Popular Magic and Folklore in Northern India*, pp. 181 ff., especially p. 191 (to avoid 'fascination' while a particularly good dinner is eaten). In our text Dhanyā leaves Saṁgama who is eating the feast prepared by herself, saṁtoṣadṛgbhayāt "because she fears that her look may 'fascinate'."

---

[11] See my 'Life of Pārśvanātha', pp. 224 ff.

[12] Read pṛchatha.

1.101: kalyāṇatā, 'happiness'. With double entente, 'golden character'.

1.103: vigalad-vasu, bahuvrīhi adjective, 'of vanishing weath', 'poor'. Cf. Whitney's *Sanskrit Grammar*, § 1299[b].

1.107: aparama, 'bereft of fortune', explained as derived from apa and ramā, 'fortune', apagatā ramā yasmāt, but really to be taken as a-parama 'he who has no superior'.

1.110: pragṛhīta, in pragṛhītābhidhāṁ bhikṣām. . .ṣaṣṭhīm 'designation of a certain form of alms'. Seven technical bhikṣās, of which this is the sixth, are listed by the comm. in a Prākrit śloka, the sixth being paggahiyā, which is explained in Sanskrit, to wit: bhojanārthaṁ karopāttabhojyamadhyād dātum iṣṭā. In the Prākrit śloka read uddhaḍā for uddhaḍă.

1.126: gajapaṭī, glossed, deśāntarīyaṁ vastram=gajavaḍiḥ (Prākrit), 'imported garment'. Cf. paṭī.

1.127: jāti-saṁsmara=jāti-saṁsmaraṇa, 'remembrance of former birth'.

1.146: tallikā, 'pool', in puṇyāmbhastallikā, 'pool of the water of virtue'; 5.47, āyallakāmbhastallikā, 'pool of the water of longing'. The latter passage is glossed: āyallako raṇaraṇaka utkaṭhā (read utkaṭā) sāivāmbhas tasya taṭākikā. Here the word āyallaka is quotable only from the Lexs. The word taṭākikā is not in the Lexs.; it glosses tallikā also at 1.146; and at 5.142, puṇyāmbhastallikā, 'pool of the water of virtue'. In 7.13, vātsalyāmṛtatallikā, 'pool of the ambrosia of kindness', the word tallikā occurs once more without gloss. For taṭākikā (otherwise unquoted) cf. the words taṭāka and taṭākinī, 'pool', 'pond'. Cf. also taḍāka, and taḍāga.

1.154: kadannakam=kadanna, 'wretched food', with pejorative syllable at the beginning and at the end.

2.3: lakṣa-dīpaka, glossed, lakṣayojanāni yāvad dīpakaḥ, 'shining to a distance of a lakh (of yojanas)'.

2.5: sapta-varṣa, 'holding seven countries', epithet of Jambūdvīpa. Gloss, atra varṣaśabdaḥ kṣetravācī. The countries are enumerated: bharata, hāimavata, harivarṣa, videha, ramyaka, āiraṇyavata (read, hāiraṇyavata), āirăvata (Lexs. only, āirāvata). See Umāsvāti's Tattvārthādhigama Sūtra 3.10 (*ZDMG* 50. 313).

2.7: pāre'bdhi, compound adverb, glossed, abdheḥ pāram. . . . avyayībhāvaḥ, 'on the other shore of the ocean (an indeclinable)'.

2.23: netra, glossed tadākhyo vṛkṣaḥ, 'name of a tree' (growing about hermitages).

2.26: śreṇi, 'supports of a king', glossed, rājñām āsthānaśreṇayo 'ṣṭādaśa. The eighteen are listed as follows: malla, āpta, hita, snigdha, mantrin, amātya, mahattama, buddhisakha, ubhayasakha, āmnāyika, sāṁgrāmika, deśīyapuruṣa, mānapuruṣa, dhanyapuruṣa, kāmapuruṣa, vijñānapuruṣa, rājapuruṣa, vinodapātrāṇi. The majority of these are not in the Lexs. Cf. the ratnāni ('jewels') of a king.

2.27: puṣkarāvarta = °vartaka, glossed, śreṣṭho meghaḥ, 'superior kind of cloud'.

2.29: bhrāmara-dhyāna, 'a kind of pious contemplation'. Glossed, vītarāgaṁ yato dhyāyan vītarāgo bhaved bhavī, ilakā bhramarībhūtā bhrāmarīdhyānato yathā (śloka).

2.73: ilopanayana, and vatsaragranthibandhana, 'sacramental practices during early childhood'.

2.77: kanaka-ghurghurāḥ, glossed, suvarṇa-ghurghurāḥ, 'golden anklets'.

2.78: keli-dolā, 'pleasure-swing'.

2.79: balakṣapakṣapakṣin, glossed rājahaṅsa, 'bright-winged bird', kenning for 'royal haṅsa'.

2.92: prabha, glossed, prakṛṣṭaṁ bhayaṁ yasyāḥ sā (qualifying prabhā, 'lustre'), 'dangerous'.

2.128: kāyavattara, glossed prakṛṣṭadeha, 'of beautiful body'.

2.134: nārī-kuñjaratā, 'condition of being elefant among women'. See lexs. s. v. nārī-kuñjara. In Pañcadaṇḍachattraprabandha, p. 28 (cf. 67), the word occurs in a different but obscure meaning.

2.135: dhoṅkāra, 'sound of a drum' = dhāuṁ-kāra, Mallinātha Caritra 4.165.

2.136: jhāṭkāra, 'sound of a lute'. Cf. jhāṁkāra (Prākrit jhaṁkāra).

3.5: kṛṣṇacitraka, glossed kālī cintāmaṇiḥ, 'black wish-jewel'. Previously, kṛṣṇaḥ citrakaḥ, in the same sense, 1.85. The word occurs also in the expression kṛṣṇacitrakakuṇḍalikā, for which see note 5 to p. 173 of Tawney's Translation of Prabandhacintāmaṇi.

3.13: apa-taru, glossed nirvṛkṣa, 'tree-less', qualifying maru, 'desert'.

3.13: daśabhid, in the passage: saṁsāre...dharmo daśabhidā bhinnaḥ kila kalpadrumāyate. Glossed, kṣāntyādinā (sc. daśabhidā). Perhaps, 'In the saṁsāra...religion, unfolded by the ten-fold unfolder, verily acts as the heavenly wish-tree'. The 'ten-fold unfolder' may be ten forms of ascetic practice (kṣānty-ādi); see Umāsvāti's Tattvārthādhigamasūtra 9.6, where the ten restraints are listed: kṣamā, mārdava, etc. In Mallinātha Caritra 3.229 the abstract daśabheda.

3.14: pākṣikatva, from pākṣika, in śukla-pākṣikatva, 'act of taking the part of pure (religion)', relating to the antithesis between śukla-dhyāna and rāudra-dhyāna. Cf. Umāsvāti 9. 29,36.

3.29: ratham-ukṣā (stem ratham-ukṣan) 'dray-steer', in the clause, rathamukṣā na gāur yathā, 'as the (male) dray-ox is not like the (female) cow'. It is not possible to construe ratham as an independent accusative. See the entire proverbial passage, p. 288.[12a]

3.30, 51: kulābhāra 'upholding the family'. Cf. kulaṁbhara.

3.34: avahīlanā, 'contempt'. Perhaps a Prākritism=Skt. avadhīraṇā. See p. 288.

3.45: tribhuvanī- in tribhuvanī-sāra (v.l. trijagatī-sāra) 'essence of the three worlds'; 4.127: tribhuvanī-nātha, 'Lord of the three worlds'. Ordinarily tribhuvana-. The form -bhuvanī-, only in composition.

3.55: gṛhā-vāsa, metrical for gṛha-vāsa 'householdership'.

3.66: pañca-mahāvratī, 'group of five great vows'. Ordinarily, mahāvrata.

3.80: trāyastriṅśa, 'designation of aids of Indra'. See Umāsvāti, 4.4. Cf. trāyodaśa, 'relating to 13'.

3.87: hṛdyaka=hṛdya, 'charm', or 'delightful gift'.

3.98: ākṛṣṭi-vidyā, 'magic charm by which one brings to one's presence'. Cf. ākṛṣṭi in Bhāvadevasūri's Pārśvanātha-caritra 1.576; and ākṛṣṭi-mantra in Lexs. An ākṛṣṭi-mantra is given in full, Divyāvadāna, p. 612 (ll. 16 ff.); the practice of ākṛṣṭi is described in Yaśodharacaritra; see Hertel, Jinakīrti's Geschichte von Pāla und Gopāla, pp. 142, 143.

[12a] But perhaps ratham is a nom., with anomalous gender: "the ox is the vehicle, not the cow" (cf. pāda b, "the he-elefant is the *herd*, not the she-elefant").—F. E.

3.125; 4.142: śvasanī-sarpa, glossed (in 4. 142), sarpaviśeṣaḥ, 'serpent that kills by breath'. Lexs. only śvasana. In Divyāvadāna, p. 105 middle, occur four kinds of serpents, one of them the present kind, śvāsa-viṣa, 'whose breath is poison.'

3.148 (bis): marud-baka, glossed, yathā marāu bakaḥ sīdati, 'heron in the wilderness'. See my paper, 'The Fable of the Crow and the Palm-Tree', *AJPh.* 40. 10.

4.9: baladhūlī, 'dust thrown up by an army, or by force', i. e., 'thick dust'. The śloka reads, samrāṭ (read °rāḍ) deveṣu bhūpāla nepālo yatra bhūbhujām, śiraḥsu baladhūlīva gandhadhūlyādhirohati. Here the word gandhadhūlī, 'musk', is reported only in Lexs. and the word baladhūlī is uncertain.

4.15: ūrṇāyu-varṇikā, 'woolen texture'. See ūrṇāyu, 'wollig' (Böhtlingk), and 'woolen blanket' (quoted from Lexs. in Mon. Will., Appendix); and varṇakā (s. v. varṇaka), 'woolen cloth' (quoted from Lexs.). Cf. ūrṇāyu-varga in 4.32.

4.30: vīra-kraya, glossed, yathākathitamūlya, 'originally stated price'.

4.32: dhāutika-rūpa, unexplained in the following two yugma stanzas: pūrṇam ūrṇāyuvargeṇa śītabhītārtirakṣaṇāiḥ, kṛtvā ca dhāutikarūpaṁ devārcāsu yad arjitaṁ; tenāgaṇyena puṇyena svajātāu prāpya ratnatām, kambalaḥ śālikāntānām aṁhrisevām ivāsadan. Seems to refer to some ascetic practice.

4.44: pārigrahika, 'pertaining to a retinue' in mantripārigrahikavigraha, 'intestine strife'.

4.62: vāhā-vṛṣabha, 'draught-bull'. Metrical for vāhă°.

4.63: dīpālaya = dīpālī, 'name of a lamp festival'; see Hertel's Translation of Hemavijaya's Kathāratnākara, vol. i, p. 97, note 3.

4.69: pratyaṅgiramahāmantramaṇḍaloddhārakarman, 'some tantric practice'. For pratyaṅgiras rites see Bloomfield, *The Atharva-Veda and the Gopatha-Brāhmaṇa*, pp. 8, 66, 68.

4.109: tritaya, 'three-fold', in bhūmi tritayī, 'threefold earth

4.120: avagāhinī, fem., 'immersing itself', 'entering'.

4.125: parībhoga, metrical for parī°, 'enjoyment'.

4.131: indra, brachylogy for indraketu, or indradhvaja, 'Indra's banner'; see p. 275 and cf. Charpentier, *Paccekabuddhageschichten*, p. 43.

4.143: yugmin. The Pet. Lexs. have, 'von unbestimmter Bedeutung', Śatruṁjayamāhātmya 3.4. The passage here reads: pitāsya.....divyabhogaśriyaṁ datte kalpadrur iva yugmināṁ,

'His father bestows upon him the bliss of divine enjoyment as the wish-tree (gives happiness) to Yugmins'. The word occurs a second time, 6.185, to wit, atisnigdhaṁ jaganmāitryā manaḥ kiṁ yugmikālavat? 'Why is their mind exceedingly tender with kindness to the world as in the time of the Yugmins?'

4.149: saṁvāhanā (caturvidhā), glossed asthi-māṅsa-tvag-roma-bhedāiś caturdhā, 'fourfold shampoo'. Lexs. have only neut. saṁvāhanam.

4.157: sormika, 'having waves'.

4.165: tala-haṭī, as gloss to adhityakā, 'table-land'. Lexs. have neither tala-haṭī, nor haṭī.

4.170: dhūma-pāka, 'smoked food'.

4.170: dvipākima, glossed, vahnisūryātapapācita, 'zwieback'.

4.173: pāṇāu-kṛta, glossed, vivāhita, 'married'. Lexs. have pāṇāu-karaṇa. Cf. pāṇi-gṛhītī, Pārśvanātha Caritra 1.570, and °gṛhītā in Kośas.

5.3: gandha-sindhura = gandhagaja, 'scent-elefant' (elefant during rut).

5.17: kekikekāyita: kekāya, 'cry kekā', as a peacock.

5.22: vinayāgastyadakṣiṇā, glossed, vinaya eva agastyas tasya nivāsāya dakṣiṇadiksamānā, 'a kind of reverence'.

5.66: ādi-potriṇī, glossed, ādi-varāhī, 'primordial she-boar'.

5.79: sapta-kṣetrī, in sapta-kṣetrī-niveśana, 'act of placing into the seven fields'. Cf. sapta-kṣetrī in 6.37 (saptāṅgīṁ saptakṣetrīm). According to Hertel, Translation of Hemavijaya's Kathāratnākara, vol i, p. 207, note 2, the seven fields are: the Monks and the Nuns; the male and female lay-disciples; the temples; the ikons of the Jinas; and the libraries of the Monks; see also vol. i, p. 232; vol. ii, p. 105, 290, and the same author's Translation of Jinakīrti's Ratnacūḍa, p. 168 (Indische Märchenromane I). The word occurs also in Mallinātha Caritra 2.658.

5.84: śrī-kalyāṇācala, glossed meruparvata, 'Mount Meru'. Cf. the mountain Śrī, mentioned frequently in Jaina literature; e. g. Bhāvadevasūri's Pārśvanāthacaritra 3.120, 124; Prabandhacintāmaṇi, Tawney's Translation, p. 10.

5.88: jagatī-dṛś, glossed jagan-netra, 'eye of the world' (sun, moon, etc.).

5.91: Gāubhadri, patronymic of Gobhadra. Neither in

Lexs. Gobhadra, however, is mentioned in Kathākośa, pp. 82, 83 of Tawney's Translation.

5.92: arvācīna-tā, glossed, ihalokāpekṣā, 'interest of the present or terrestrial world'.

5.94: kubja, glossed, tṛṇa-kuṭīraka, 'grass hut'.

5.97: taptāyogola-kalpa, 'age of the heated fire-ball', 'present age'.

5.103: uddhukṣita, glossed, dagdha, 'kindled'. Root dhukṣ, otherwise only in composition with sam.

5.105: trasa-rekhā, 'floating line in jewels', in the expression, trasarekheva ratneṣu mahāmahimahānaye, 'as a floating line in a jewel, calculated to diminish worth'. See p. 289.

5.109: susthitaka-prāya, 'for the most part unshaken', but with pun on 'some brilliant headgear worn by a king', parallel to kalyāṇa-māuli (glossed, suvarṇamukuṭa). susthitaka is glossed by Prākrit sūthiyā, lokabhāṣāyāṁ īḍhuṇī, quotable neither from Hemacandra, nor Pischel's Index. The passage reads: kalyāṇamāulāu śrīvīrasvāmyādeśe śiraḥsthite, kathaṁ susthitakaprāyaṁ rājate rājaśāsanam. The susthitaka is, apparently, a headdress inferior to the diadem (māuli).

5.120: sakala-devāḥ, glossed svayaṁbhūdevatānām, saprabhavānāṁ vā, 'superior gods'. Mallinātha Caritra 7.574 has devatā sakalā.

5.131: phālikā, in, katham...karpūraphālikābhir prāsādaśikharaṁ bhavet, perhaps, 'how can the crest of a palace be made out of slabs of camfor?' phālikā seems to be a vṛddhi-derivative from phalaka.

5.134: vijigāhiṣu, 'desiring to immerse one's self'.

5.138: devadantin, glossed āirāvaṇa, 'Indra's elefant'. In Lexs. said to be Śiva (erroneously).

5.150: tuṇḍa-tāṇḍava, glossed, mukhanṛtyam, 'mouth-dance', i. e., 'vain talk'.

5.153: udvāma, perhaps "emission"? In the cpd. nisvānodvāmasāṁrāviṇe; see p. 289 above. The gloss renders nisvānodvāma- by ravād bhayānake.

6.11: nāsīravīratā, 'position of a hero in the van of an army'.

6.22: vy-amrākṣīt, from vi+mṛś, glossed, preṣayāmāsa, 'dismissed'.

6.41: maṇī-maya, metrical for maṇī- 'jeweled'. maṇī is quoted as an independent stem, Ādīśvara Caritra, 2.22: see

Suali, 'L'Ādīśvaracaritram', *Studi Italiani di Filologia Indo-Iranica*, vol. 7, p. 6.

6.50: lañkha, glossed vaṁśāgrādinṛtyādikārin. Seems to mean, 'some kind of acrobat or dancer'. In the dvandva compound lañkha-mañkha-vidūṣakān, the two last members of which are glossed respectively, mañkhāś citraphalakahastāḥ, and vidūṣakā ūmakadūcakādivācakāḥ (kad-ūcaka = kad-vada, not in Lexs.).

6.64: adevadru, 'without devadāru trees'. Neither devadru nor adevadru in the Lexs.

6.79: lūkā, glossed lokoktyā "lū". The śloka reads: yatra dehe nṛpaśvāsāiḥ śūcīsūcā prapañcitā (gloss, śūcikakalpanā kathitā), lūkā jhalajhalā tatra malayānilatāṁ gatā. Once more lūkā in 7.142: vyāmohena mahāhimena mathitaṁ no māyayā lūkayā kopena prabalātapena na madāi rogābhiyogāir iva. This lūkā with its colloquial lū seems to run parallel to yūka and yū 'louse'. The word is evidently pejorative, but I do not venture to guess its meaning.

6.81: kiṭṭita-lohatā, glossed kīṭalohatā, would seem to mean, 'red color of some insect'. Or, is kiṭṭita denominal participle from kiṭṭa 'rust', so that the compound means 'rusty color'? In antithesis with gāurikatā, 'color of white mustard.'

6.82: kāntalohapātra, glossed kāntīlohabhājanam, kāntīlohabhājano 'gnitāpena dugdham utphaṇatīti lokoktiḥ (ut-phaṇ, not in Lexs.). The Lexs. have kāntalāuha = lohakānta-'magnetic iron'.

6.85: vāiśvānara-rathyā, glossed agnisamānamārga, 'a particular division of the moon's path' = vāiśvānara-patha.

6.89: dhūpanī, fem., ordinarily dhūpana, neut., 'exhalation'.

6.95: uttuṇḍa, glossed utpāṭitamukha, 'with open snout', (said of jackals).

6.103: bhadra, mahābhadra, sarvatobhadra, yavamadhyā, and vajramadhyā, 'certain kinds of Jaina ikons'. Gloss: etāḥ sarvāḥ pratimāviśeṣāḥ.

6.116, 141: trilokītilaka, 'ornament of the three worlds'.

6.137: kīradāru, glossed, kīrakāṣṭha, 'designation of a tree'.

6.155: dvādaśābdīya, glossed, dvādaśābdānāṁ samāhāraḥ, abdāni varṣāṇi, 'period of twelve years'.

6.156: manorathika, 'springing from desire'

6.158: savana-pīṭha, glossed, snāna-pīṭha, 'bath-stool'. The latter word in this sense 4.151. Neither compound in the Lexs.

6.194: abdhijalamānuṣī, glossed jalavāsinī strī, 'mermaid'.

6.205: īryāpāthikī = āiryā°, q.v.

7.18: vi-sādhaya-, 'achieve'.

7.26: alpa-kālīna, in antithesis with śāśvata, 'of short duration'.

7.32: rādhā-vedhas, neuter, 'act of shooting so as to hit the aim'; cf. -vedhin, and -bhedin. See Merutuñga's Prabandhacintāmaṇi, pp. 45, 77 of Tawney's Translation. According to Leumann in a note to p. 45 of Tawney's work, Rādhā is a puppet (Prākrit puttaliyā), painted into the middle of a butt, as a mark to shoot at. He who hits it is a rādhā-vedhin. On p. 45 the word Rādhā is inverted into Dhārā, the name of a courtezan.

7.33: netra-paṭṭa, glossed, deśāntarāyātavastraviśeṣam, 'imported garment'.

7.36: pañcāñgirakṣaṇa, glossed, sādhukṛtyā, 'paḍilehīkarī', 'some Jain practice'; in juxtaposition with pañcanamaskāra, 'reverence to the Arhats, etc.'

7.38: pādapopagama = pādapopagamana (nāmānaśanam), 'death by fast under a tree'.

7.60: korita, as gloss to utkīrṇa, 'heaped'. Dhātupāṭha has a root kur 'utter a sound', which does not suit.

7.94: vāsī-candana-kalpa, describing an advanced ascetic, 'he to whom the (burning) sword and the (cooling) sandal are all the same'. This word occur in Buddhist Sanskrit. See the author, *JAOS* 40. 339 ff. The antithesis between sandal and sword occurs also in Prabandhacintāmaṇi; see p. 92 of Tawney's Translation; and cf. Böhtlingk, Indische Sprüche 4882.

7.118: cūlā = cūḍā, 'crest'.

Appendix iv: Words quoted only in Lexicons or Grammars, or quoted in their present meaning only in the same class of texts.

The Śālibhadra Carita, in common with many other Jaina texts, uses many words and expressions which are recorded hitherto only in the native Lexicons and Grammars. Beginning with the great and prolific Hemacandra, the Jainas were ardent students of filology. In the Mallavādi Prabandha, the scarcely less famous Haribhadrasūri says of himself that his belly is so full of learning (śāstrapūrāt) as to threaten to burst, and that he is, therefore, tying it with a golden band. If he should happen not to understand the sense of a single word spoken by any one, he vows to become his pupil. See Candraprabhasūri's Prabhāvaka Carita, pp. 104 bottom; 105 top. The same, or similar, statements appear in Māṇikyasūri's Yaśodhara Carita, and in a Paṭṭāvalī, extracted in Weber's *Handschriftenverzeichniss*, ii. 3, p. 1034 (nr. 1989); see Hertel, *Jinakīrti's Geschichte von Pāla und Gopāla*, pp. 142, 144[13]. The monk Śobhana[14] studies for twelve years not only Grammars, Lexicons, and Poetics, but also other sciences, in the 138th story of Hemavijaya's Kathāratnākara (Hertel's Translation, vol. ii, p. 81).[15] Inasmuch, therefore, as Jaina texts are all relatively late, it does not follow that words which occur in them, and only Kośa and Vyākaraṇa texts besides, are any more 'quotable' than the grammatical forms of the Bhaṭṭikāvya. Thus maṇḍala (maṇḍalaka), cited widely by Lexicografers in the sense of 'dog', occurs in that sense in Pārśvanātha 3.1104; Dharmaparīkṣā 2.36; 4.74 (Mironow, p. 8), but we may not, therefore alone, assume that the word is really Sanskrit[16]. Nay, even if the word in that sense should ultimately turn up in 'Classical' Sanskrit literature, we should not be certain that the Jaina authors actually knew it as such: it would still be possible, or rather likely, that their knowledge of it is derived solely from the Kośas. The same caution should attend our judgment of many Jaina words. Thus, e. g., ajākṛpaṇīya, Śālibhadra 5.125; Hemavijaya's Kathāratnākara, story 19 (Hertel's Translation, vol. i, p. 54), in the sense of 'unexpected untoward happening'. This Pāṇinean word, as yet unquoted in Sanskrit literature proper, is the precise opposite

---

[13] Cf. Winternitz, *Geschichte der Indischen Litteratur*, 2. 320.

[14] For Śobhana see Tawney, Translation of Prabandhacintāmaṇi, p. 62. Cf. Winternitz, l. c., p. 341.

[15] Cf. the droll story in Prabandhacintāmaṇi, p. 39, where an entire family, down to the wretched one-eyed maid-servant, is clever enough to fill in stanzas partly recited before them (samasyā, dodhaka, or gūḍhacaturthaka). That was, doubtless, a Jaina family.

[16] This word is also Prākrit, but that does not explain its origin, nor is it likely that the Sanskrit writers have borrowed it from that source; see Zachariae, *Beiträge zur Indischen Lexicographie*, p. 66.

of kākatālīya, 'unexpected favorable happening', which is very common in Sanskrit; see the author, *AJPh.* 40. 11 ff. Tho ajākṛpaṇīya refers to a well-known apolog, and is probably good Sanskrit, the Jaina writers seem to derive it from Pāṇini, and not from any literary source hitherto unrevealed.

Quite certainly Pradyumnasūri, the learned, elegant, and fecund author or redactor of the present Śālibhadra Carita, does derive part of his verbal inspiration directly from the Grammarians. Thus we have stanzas 5.44, 45:

> tad ahaṁ *sāsahiḥ* kaṣṭaṁ *vāvahir* bhāram āhitam,
> *cācalis* tava nirdeśāir apakīrtāu na *pāpatiḥ;*
> bhujiṣyas te yatiṣye 'haṁ sarvārthaprāptaye tathā,
> labdhvā[17] yathāham indratvaṁ gosvāmī na vyathiṣyate.

The Body speaks to the Mind: 'Then I (the Body), bravely enduring hardships, stoutly bearing the burden imposed upon me, swift to obey thy orders, not plunging into disrepute—may I, as thy (Mind's)servant, thus strive to fulfil thy every intention, so that thou, my Master, after having obtained control, shalt not fail of thy purpose'. The four italicized reduplicated adjectives (participles) appear *in the same order* in Pāṇini 5.2.38. It does not matter that three of them (all but pāpati) are from Rig-Vedic times, whereas pāpati is cited only by Grammarians; our author obviously derived them from Pāṇini, and their individual chronology is negligible, in so far as our author's diction is concerned.

Once more, at Śālibhadra 4.50, occur three adjectives in -āyya in the following śloka:

> śrī*nikāyya*[18] *praṇāyyo*[19] 'pi kambalaḥ prājya*prāyya*bhūḥ[20]
> prasahya mahyam ānāyya sapradarpaṁ samarpyatām.

The passage is spoken by Queen Cellaṇā to King Śreṇika: 'O (king), dwelling-house of Fortune! bring here by force, and proudly give me the shawl which, tho it be (intrinsically) worthless, confers great honor!' The theme of the command of the queen is a shawl of magic power. The three italicized words above are all from Pāṇini 3.1.138; our author's use of them throws not

---

[17] Text, erroneously, labdhā.

[18] Glossed, lakṣmīgṛha.

[19] Glossed, asaṁmata.

[20] Glossed, bahumānakāraṇam.

the least light on their standing in literature. They may, or they may not, be mere fictions of grammar, as far as Pradyumnasūri's testimony goes.

Less stringent, yet quite convincing, is the alliterating use of the words āśvīna and adyaśvīna in 5.46.

dehavāhamanaḥsādisāṅgatyam avagamya tat,
sa mene bhavam āśvīnam adyaśvīnaṁ jayotsavam.

'Having understood this connection of the Mind seated in the vehicle of the Body, (Śālibhadra) regarded existence as a victorious race, run by a horse in one day (āśvīna)[21], coming to an end to-day or to-morrow (adya-śvīna)[22]. The two glossed words are cited respectively in Pāṇini 5.2.19 and 5.2.13; there is scarcely a chance that our author knew them from literature or any source of information other than that of the Grammarians.

The two curious compounded gerunds, kaṇe-hatya and mano-hatya[23] occur in 5.26 and 6.165 respectively in the sense of 'being sated or satisfied' (glossed, tṛpti-paryantam, and tṛpti-sūcakam). Pāṇini treats these anomalous verbal prefixes (gati) in 1.4.66, 3.1.6. I take it unquestioningly that Pradyumnasūri has derived them from grammar, and not from any other source.

'The Grammarians teach that any noun-stem in the language may be converted without any other addition than that of an *a* into a present stem' (Whitney, *Skt. Gramm.* 1054). Such forms occur scatteringly thru the language, and Jaina writers seem to favor them. Thus our text, 1.118, has suvarṇati, 'to be worth gold', glossed, suvarṇāyate (neither in the Lexs.); 6.95, kāntāsaṁgītanti, glossed, kāntāsaṁgītam ivācaranti, 'they practice the song of female loves'. The word is used of the howl of open-mouthed she-jackals (uttuṇḍacaṇḍapheraṇḍāḥ, glossed, utpāṭitamukhavac caṇḍaśṛgālyaḥ); 7.80, vajrati, 'be hard as adamant', glossed, vajra ivācarati. Suali, in his 'Analisi dell' Ādīśvaracaritra di Hemacandra,' *Studi Italiani di Filologia Indo-Iranica*, vol. 7, p. 6, cites the forms paśavanti, 2.973, and, cañcarīkanti, 5.402. It seems as tho this fenomenon, whose scope it is not possible as yet to state, is due to acquaintance with grammar, rather than to inspiration from outside literary models.

---

[21] Glossed, āsvīno 'dhvā sa yo 'śvena dinenāikena gamyate.

[22] Glossed, adya śvo vā bhavam adyaśvīnam.

[23] Not in the Lexs.

The same is true of occasional Vedisms in Jaina Sanskrit. Our text, 6.188, has the reduplicated participial adjective, governing the accusative, dadhi (glossed, dadhāti), quoted only from Veda and Grammarians. In the same śloka occurs nir-īyamāṇayoḥ (glossed, nirgachatoḥ) which is also pretty clearly a Vedic archaism. In 1.79, the participle eṣantyāḥ (glossed, āgachantyāḥ) is quotable only from RV. and AV. In 5.13 we have rājasarpaḥ prasarpantaṁ yakaṁ jegilyate...bhogilokam, 'the anaconda (with double entente, 'royal serpent', meaning King Śreṇika) who devours the poor serpent-folk (with double entente, 'his happy people')'. The pejorative or diminutive use of suffix ka with pronoun is essentially Vedic; see Edgerton, *JAOS* 31. 93ff., but is occasionally found in Jaina texts, see my 'Life of Pārśvanātha', p. 238. See also, as instances of real diminutives in our text, 5.108, naraka (glossed, kutsito naraḥ), 'unworthy man'; and, 5.126, pūtaraka, from pūtara, 'despised insect'; cf. kadannakam, above. Nevertheless yaka may be a mere Vedism. Mironow, *Die Dharmaparīkṣā*, p.7 ff., cites from that text, anāśvāṅs, 'not having eaten'; viśvajanīna, 'ruler of all folk'; aśanāyā, 'hunger'; caraṇyu, kenning for 'wind'. We may feel sure that some of these Vedic words are derived from filological rather than literary sources. So probably also the nominative nā, 'man' (stem nṛ) in Mahāvīra Carita 1.136.

The following is an additional list of words quoted only in Lexicons or Grammars, or quoted in their present meaning only in the same class of texts; it contains more than forty words, in addition to those discussed in the preceding.

1.38: utpaśya, 'looking up or upwards'. Glossed, unmukha. Also in Mallinātha Caritra 6.244.

1.40: sahya, 'health' (gloss, sahyāya = nīrogāya).

1.65: dhūmarī, 'mist', 'fog'; see Zachariae, l. c., pp. 55, 66.

1.77: kuṇḍalikā, 'mixture of rice and ghee' = kuṇḍala. This sense of kuṇḍalikā is not given in the Lexs.

1.93: śilāputra, 'good-for-nothing'. The interesting gloss reads:

nirbhāgyo durbhagaḥ paṅguḥ kuṇiḥ kuṇṭhamatis tathā,
nīcaḥ pāparato yas tu śilāputraḥ sa ucyate.

kecid evam āhuḥ: kasyāś cit striyo loḍhako jātas tayāsāv araṇye tyaktaḥ (accordingly loḍhaka seems to mean 'bantling', to be exposed in the forest). kuṇṭha-matis (not in Lexs.) = kuṇṭha-manas, 'weak-minded'. Mallinātha 7.393 has aśmaputra in the same sense.

1.96: pātratrā-kṛ, glossed, pātrāya dīyata iti pātratrā; "deye trā ca" (Pāṇini 7.2.133), 'to give to a worthy person'.

1.115; 4.163: āśitaṁbhava, glossed, tṛpti, 'satiety'; only in Pāṇini and Lexs.

1.117: praguṇāir guṇāiḥ is glossed by āudanikāir guṇāiḥ. The word āudanika is quoted only in Gaṇa saṁtāpādi, to Pāṇ. 5.1.101. The reference of the scholiast is to the word puṇyapāka in the text, so that the meaning of āudanika, 'one who knows how to cook porridge', is relevant.

1.125; 7.2; Mallinātha Caritra, 8.466: aṣaḍakṣīṇa, glossed, catuṣkarṇa, 'not seen by six eyes', i. e., 'known by two persons only', 'secret', Pāṇ. 5.4.7. Cf. the familiar ṣaṭkarṇa, as contrasted with catuṣkarṇa in parallel senses, and see the author in *Proceedings of the American Philosophical Society*, vol. 56, p. 13.

2.33: caturā, glossed hastiśālā, 'elefants' stable'. The neuter caturam occurs in that sense in the Lexs. only.

2.55, 56: tāilakanda and tāilakanda-mahāratnam, 'crystal', or 'jewel', glossed, amṛtakuṇḍasamaṁ tāilakandanāmnā ratnaviśeṣaḥ; and, sphaṭikaratnaviśeṣaḥ. The word is quoted in the Lexs. only in the sense of 'a certain bulb'.

2.66: pātrīṇa, in sarva-pātrīṇa, glossed, sarvapātrebhyo yogyāni, 'filling the whole dish', 'abundant'.

2.73: The word riṅṣaṇam is to be emended to riñkhaṇam, 'crawling', and is so quoted only in Lexs.

2.93: lakṣmīpuṣpa, glossed, padmarāgamaṇi, 'ruby'.

2.128: ciraṇṭīkāś (emend, ciraṇṭikāś) ciraṇṭīḥ (the latter glossed, vadhūṭyāḥ), apparently, 'a class of women described in the Kāmasūtra'. The Lexs. s. vs. ciraṇṭī, ciriṇṭī, 'a woman, married or single, who, after maturity, resides in her father's house'. Only in Lexs. and Gramm.—ciraṇṭī also in 4.36; ciraṇṭikā, glossed by vadhū, also in 6.140.

3.6: bhādramātura, glossed, bhadrā mātā yasyāsāu, 'son of a virtuous or handsome mother'. Here with double entente, Bhadrā being Śāli's mother.

3.8: cidrūpa, glossed, paṇḍita, 'wise'. In that sense only in Lexs.

3.15; 6.52: yāpyayāna, glossed, śivikā, 'palanquin', 'litter'. The same word in 6.7 (glossed sukhāsana). The Sanskrit form is a facile, yet really senseless, folk-etymological back-formation of Prākrit jhaṁpāṇa; see Zachariae, in *Vienna Oriental Journal* vol. 16, p. 25.

3.70: hiṇḍi, glossed, rātrāu rakṣācāra, 'night-watch'.

3.80: kukṣiṁ-bhari, 'gluttonous'.

4.7: kāutaskuta, glossed, kutaḥkuto bhavāḥ, 'coming from an unknown country'; Mallinātha Caritra 5.93. The feminines kāutaskutā and kāutaskutī, Mal. 6.390; 7.576. Quoted in Gaṇa kaskādi. Cf. kāutastya, 'coming whence', Pārśvanātha 3.618; Mal. 1.52.

4.9: gandhadhūli, 'musk'.

4.23: galakambala, 'bull's dewlap'. Lexs. and Uṇādisūtra. See Hemavijaya's Kathāratnākara, Hertel's Translation, vol. ii, pp. 156, 271.

4.66: ciratna, 'ancient'. Pāṇini and Grammarians. Digest, in the Introduction to the text, glosses, ciraṁtana.

4.142: ku-rājya, 'evil government'.

4.153: jāñgulīya, glossed, gāruḍika, 'snake-charmer'. Lexs. have jāñguli etc. in that sense.

4.162: panīpatyate, intensive from pat. Only in Gramm.

4.166: hayapriya, glossed, yava, 'barley'.

5.47: āyallaka, 'longing', in āyallakāmbhastallikā, 'pool of the water of longing'.

5.49: kalā-keli, glossed, kandarpa, 'sporting with the digits of the moon', as a kenning of Kāma.

5.116: varṇikā, 'purity of gold'; see Lexs., s. v. varṇaka.

6.36: vīra-jayantikā, glossed, vīra-patākā, 'hero-flag'.

6.43: somāla in su-somāla, 'very delicate'. Cf. 6.118, where the text has somā latā, for somālatā, 'delicacy'.

6.87: bhissā and bhissaṭā, 'inferior kinds of cooked rice'.

6.92: karpūra-pāñcālī, 'puppet made of camfor'. pāñcālī, in that sense, only in Lexs. (frequent in Vikrama Carita, F.E.); it is glossed by pūtalī, not in Lexs., and doubtless = puttalī. Cf. puttikā.

6.94: kaṭūtkaṭā, 'dried ginger'.

6.94: aṭāṭyā, '(habit of) roaming'.

6.97: avāvarī, fem. of adj. avāvan, glossed, oṇṛ apanayane, āuṇati doṣān, 'carrying off (blemishes)'. Pāṇini and Lexs.

6.191: kātyāyanī, glossed, ardhavṛddhanārī, 'middle-aged woman'. Also in Prabandhacintāmaṇi; see p. 34 of Tawney's Translation.

7.4: kukkuṭa-grāma, glossed kugrāma, 'low caste village'. kukkuṭa = kukkura, 'offspring of a Niṣāda by a Śūdra woman'. Only Lexs.

7.5: mañjī = mañjā, glossed ajā, 'she-goat'. Both only in Lexs.

7.18: varkara, glossed, hāsyena ajāputreṇa vā, 'sport', or, 'kid'. In the former sense only in Lexs.

7.27: kalamba, glossed, bāṇa, 'arrow'.

7.57: kīl, 'bind', in jāla-kīlita, 'caught in a net'.

7.87: nir-vīra, glossed, niṣpatisutā, 'woman without husband and sons'. In this sense only in Lexs.

7.138: śākhāpura, glossed, purasya samīpaṁ yad upapuram, 'suburb' = śākhānagara.

Appendix v: Denominal Verbs and Participles: Elative Verbs in tarām.

In my 'Life of Pārśvanātha', p. 230 ff., I have listed a notably large number of new denominal formations. This seems to me to be a peculiarity of Jaina diction, for the present text also exhibits considerable fertility in this respect; see Suali's parallel observation on the text of the Ādīśvaracaritra, l. c., p. 6. In addition to the denominals in -a, mentioned above, p. 309, Śālibhadra Carita contributes the following list:

1.2: ghṛtameghāyita, 'acted as a cloud rich in ghee'. The passage is, ādāu dhanabhāve yena ghṛtameghāyitam. Gloss, ghṛtameghavad ācaritam. In 6.203 occur further the parallel compounds dugdhameghāyita, mahāmeghāyita, dadhimeghāyita, and sudhāmeghāyita. The uncompounded denominative meghāya- is familiar, but these participles are denominals made directly from compounds.

1.15: sajjanāya-, 'to act a good part'.

1.96: cintāmaṇīya-, 'to act the part of a thought-gem'.

1.157: svāmīya-, 'to rule'.

2.121: vasanta-samayāyita, 'pervaded by the spring season'.

The passage is, puṣpaprakaranikṣepāir vasantasamayāyitam, (sc. vīvāham[!], in stanza 126), 'a wedding turned into spring season by throwing bouquets of flowers'.

2.122: suparva-nagarāyita 'turned into a festive city'. The passage is, divyāir dūṣyāir alaṁkārāiḥ suparva-nagarāyitam, (sc. vīvāham), 'a wedding turned into a city festival by means of divine garments and ornaments'. Followed by another denominal participle, koṇita, in the expression nāyavallīdalāiḥ pūgapūgāiḥ[24] kāuñkaṇakoṇitam (sc. vīvāham). Here kāuñkaṇakoṇitam is obscure.

3.13: kalpadrumāya-, 'act as the wish-tree', cf. śaṭatpattradrumāyate, 'become tree with falling leaves', Pārśvanātha Caritra 2.177.

3.28: ālānaya-, 'fasten to an elefant's post'.

6.55: pari-cīvarita, 'drest in a ragged monk's garment'.

6.63: vimukhāyita, 'averted'; gloss, vimukhacārita.

6.69: tūrṇaya-, 'to make restless'; glossed, utsukīkuryāt.

6.69: apakarṇita, glossed, avagaṇita, 'disregarded'.

6.186: svargasargāyita, where sargāyita has the gloss, sṛṣṭi, 'there was created heaven'.

7.129: saṁdhīraya (text, sandhī°), 'encourage'.

I add here, as established Jaina usage, tho not restricted to these texts, the frequent employment of the elative suffix tarām to finite verbs: 2.105, plāvayate-tarām; 4.141; 5.115, dodūyate-tarām; 5.53, rocate-tarām; 6.93, paprathire-tarām; 6.159, tatvarire-tarām; 6.191, mumude-tarām. Cf. my 'Life of Pārśvanātha', p. 238.

Appendix vi: Emendations and Corrections.

1.2: for yathorvīśasyaśrīḥ, read °śasya śrīḥ.

1.19: for jañgamas sevadhis, read °maś śevadhiḥ. But sevadhi also in 2.55.

1.26: for nicchadmā (glossed, nirmāyā), read niśchadmā, 'unprotected'; or, possibly, niḥṣadmā, 'without abode' (anyasadmasu niḥṣadmā, in alliteration).

1.52: in the note 9 on the stanza read in the gloss, āveśinyo for aveśinyo.

---

[24] Glossed, kramuka-samahāiḥ, meaning °samūhāiḥ.

1.57: for pṛcchata, read pṛcchatha.
1.68: for °tandulān, read °taṇḍulān. So also in 5.107.
1.69, note 9: for sarkarām, read śarkarām.
1.71: for prativeśanyaḥ, read prativeśinyaḥ, as in the repeated śloka 1.124.
2.5, note: for āiraṇyavata, read hāiraṇyavata.
2.73: for riṅṣanam, read riñkhanam.
2.80: for śūkaraḥ, read sū°.
2.122, note 3: for kramukasamahāiḥ, read °samūhāiḥ.
2.128: for ciraṇṭīkāś, read ciraṇṭīkāś.
2.140: for nacāstamitam, read na cā°.
3.46: Separate the two vocatives, anutsuka and mahotsāha, which are printed as one word.
4.9: for samrāṭ, read samrāḍ.
4.10: the alternate reading, kambalāiḥ svabalāir iva, is to be taken into the text.
4.21: for kiṁ balaṁ, read kiṁbalaṁ.
4.43: for vāttapitta°, read vātapitta°.
4.67: for kiṁ rūpaḥ, read kiṁrūpaḥ.
4.118: for śṛṇi-śūcyeva, read sṛṇi-sūcyeva.
4.153: for jāñgulīyapadena vā, read jāñgulīyapadeneva (?).
4.156: for sūresu read śūresu. This particular interchange between ś and s is a frequent Jainism; see e. g. Hertel, *Indische Märchen*, p. 130.
5.7: punarāvṛtā seems to stand for °vṛttā, 'recurring'.
5.45: for labdhā, read labdhvā.
5.47: in gloss 5 read utkaṭā, for utkaṭhā.
5.61: for harmyiaṇām, read harmyāṇām.
5.80: in tvam api pūraya sarvāñgacañgasarvāśāḥ, separate °cañga from sarvāśāḥ, 'having knowledge of all Añgas, fulfil thou all hopes'. With double entente, 'do thou of sound limbs, fill all the regions of space'.
5.103: for parādeśānalāi mātar, read parādeśānalāir mātar.
5.107: for °tandulāḥ read °taṇḍulāḥ. So also in 1.68.
5.111: for nānārūpī cakre, read nānārūpīcakre.
5.119: for nyatkāra (gloss, tiraskāra), read nyak-kāra.
6.17: for tad duḥkhato, read tadduḥkhato.
6.18: for somā latā, read somālatā, 'delicacy'.
6.43: for sukhamāmūlāiḥ, read suṣamāmūlāiḥ.

6.54: for bhūṣaṇānyastadūṣaṇaḥ, read bhūṣaṇān nyastadūṣaṇaḥ. The rare masculine bhūṣaṇān also in 6.56.

6.93: for svāmisattāyā, read svāmisaktāyā.

6.110: for kīkāśa°, read kīkāsa°.

6.174: for pravrajiṣyāmaḥ, read the conditional prāvrajiṣyāmaḥ.

7.3: for parāvṛttya, read, perhaps, parāvartya. But Jaina texts seem to confuse primary and causative forms a good deal; see Weber, Pañcadaṇḍachattraprabandha, p. 3; and my 'Life of Pārśvanātha', p. 238.

7.63: for nīrajanirañjana, read, perhaps, nīraja nirañjana, pace gloss kamalavan nirañjana.

7.80: for triparīkṣitavajrati, read triparīkṣitaṁ vajrati.

7.96: for mṛgapakṣigaṇākulām read °kulā, agreeing with the subject of the sentence.

7.122: for mahāśamarasaṁrambhe, read mahāsamara°, with pun, to be sure, on mahāśama-rasaṁ rambhe; see p. 262.

7.176, note 2: for vidhāpyate, read vidhyāpyate; see my remarks on the 'root' vidhyā, 'Life of Pārśvanātha', p. 220, and cf. above, p. 296.

In 5.53; 6.122 we have the frase, mṛṣṭaṁ vāidyopadiṣṭaṁ ca, 'delicacies and food prescribed by fysicians'. The same frase is printed in 4.81 as miṣṭaṁ vāidyopadiṣṭaṁ ca. Tho both mṛṣṭam and miṣṭam are good Sanskrit[25], only one of these (here mṛṣṭam) should appear in a given text.

[25] miṣṭam is perhaps a cross between mṛṣṭam and iṣṭam, under Prākritic impulse.

www.ingramcontent.com/pod-product-compliance
Lightning Source LLC
Chambersburg PA
CBHW022030080426
42733CB00007B/780
9783741166273